THE

DORSET

YEAR BOOK

FOR 2015

ONE HUNDRED AND SIXTH YEAR OF ISSUE

First published in Great Britain in 2014 by The Society of Dorset Men

Copyright © 2014 The Society of Dorset Men

A CIP catalogue record for this book is available from the British Library.

Paperback ISBN 978-0-9926594-1-7
Price £6.00

Edited by Trevor Vacher-Dean

Printed and bound in Great Britain by
Print Team (Dorset) Limited
www.printteam.co.uk

Our Cover: DORCHESTER by Arthur Cecil Fare - the artist featured in this Year Book
Published with the kind permission of Frank Herring and Sons Ltd
Arts and Craft Centre, Dorchester, who commissioned the original painting.
Mounted prints of this watercolour, at £20 each are available from their High West Street premises.

CONTENTS

THE SOCIETY OF DORSET MEN

FOUNDED JULY 7th, 1904

'A Silver Tower Dorset Red Banner Bears'

President:
LORD FELLOWES OF WEST STAFFORD, DL

Deputy Presidents:
SIR ANTHONY JOLLIFFE, GBE, DL, D.Sc, D.Mus
JEREMY POPE, OBE, DL

Hon. Deputy President:
GORDON E. HINE, FRICS
ROY ADAM, MBE

Past Presidents:
SIR FREDERICK TREVES, BART, GCVO, CB, LLD, 1904 - 1907
THOMAS HARDY, OM, LITT.D, JP, 1907 - 1909
COLONEL JOHN MOUNT BATTEN, CB, 1909 - 1911
COLONEL SIR ROBERT WILLIAMS, BART, VD, 1911 - 1913
SIR STEPHEN COLLINS, JP, 1913 - 1915
JOHN CASTLEMAN SWINBURNE-HANHAM, JP, 1915 - 1919
THE RIGHT HON. The EARL of SHAFTESBURY, KP, PC, GCVO, 1919 - 1922, 1924 - 1925
CAPTAIN THE RIGHT HON. F. E. GUEST, CBE, DSO, 1922 - 1924
CAPTAIN ANGUS V. HAMBRO, DL, JP, 1925-33, 1936 - 1944
LIEUT.-COL. SIR PHILIP COLFOX, BART, MC, 1933 - 1936
H.E. THE RIGHT HON. LORD LLEWELLIN, CBE, MC, TD, DL, 1944 - 1957
BRIGADIER G. M. B. PORTMAN, CB, TD, DL, 1957 - 1961
ROBERT TOM WARREN, 1962 - 1963
COLONEL SIR RICHARD GLYN, BART, OBE, TD, DL, 1964 - 1969
SIMON WINGFIELD DIGBY, MA, TD, DL, 1970 - 1984
SIR ANTHONY JOLLIFFE, GBE, DL, D.Sc, D.Mus, 1984 - 2011

Past Hon. Secretaries:
WILLIAM WATKINS, JP, 1904 - 1925
H. LL. WATKINS, 1925 - 1937
S . H. J. DUNN, 1937 - 1940
E. G. GALE, 1940 - 1941
HARRY J. HARVEY, 1941 - 1942
F. C. H. DENNETT, AACCA, FRES, 1942 - 1961
W. T. G. PERROTT, MIWO, 1961 - 1969
J. C. R. PREWER, 1969 - 1979
G. E. HINE, FRICS, 1979 - 2004

Past Hon. Editors:
SIR NEWMAN FLOWER, 1914 - 1920
STANLEY L. GALPIN, 1920 - 1932
H. LL. WATKINS, 1935 - 1937
ASHLEY C. ROGERS, 1937 - 1950
FRANK C. H. DENNETT, 1951 - 1960
N. J. ('NAT') BYLES, 1961 - 1978
FRED LANGFORD, 1979 - 1994
GEORGE LANNING, 1995 - 2000
PETER PITMAN, 2001 - 2013

The 2015 YEAR BOOK - a dip-in digest of Dorset delights

Anecdotes, biographies, matters historic and current, serious features, humorous interludes, detailed specialist reports, poetry, articles to give you pause, things to make you chuckle and things to make you weep.

It is our largest edition in over 30 years and all contributions were gratefully received but some, through lack of space, have been held in reserve. To extend the existing subject range, articles on music, sport, hobbies, media and the environment are solicited for next year and beyond.

To forge closer links between our organisations and to mark the new Society of Dorset Men history display, county members will each receive a bookmark with their Year Book. This has a tear-off **free entry ticket** to the wonderful Dorset County Museum in Dorchester. Read all about its marvels in the comprehensive feature starting on page 84. A visit will take at least two hours and makes a terrific family outing. Remember, of course, that free entry covers only the Society member.

Please inform the Editor of special achievements by, or awards granted to, our members. Personal, professional, social or other accomplishments should be lauded and reported in the Year Book as items of great interest to our readers and permanent records for future research.

Congratulations to Allan Cooper of Wimborne St. Giles who, in acknowledgement of annual contributions to the Year Book since 1958, has been granted Life Membership of our Society.

Any ideas or suggestions to improve the Dorset Year Book or to enhance the Society of Dorset Men and its activities are always welcome. More over-all support is needed from members, particularly for social events. The Year Book has been produced for you. Please enjoy it.

YEAR BOOK CONTACTS

Editorial: Trevor Vacher-Dean
Rosslyn Cottage, 8 Love Lane, Weymouth. DT4 8JZ
Tel: 01305 781261 E-mail: vacherdean@yahoo.co.uk

Advertising: Stuart Adam
Court Barton, West Bagber, Taunton, Somerset. TA4 3EQ
Tel: 01823 432076 E-mail: stu.adam@outlook.com

Sales & Distribution: Andy Hutchings
23 Hereford Road, Weymouth. DT4 OQB
Tel: 01305 784332 E-mail: a.hutchings265@btinternet.com

When e.mailing, in the first instance, please also give your postal address.
Please be patient — as volunteers we are not always 'on call'
but pledge to respond as quickly as possible.

Thinker, Sailor, Soldier, Hoarder, Breadman, Headman, Short Man, Chief. . . .

Peter St. John Tubbs remembers his grandfather

ALBERT Newman joined the Royal Navy at the age of 15 and served his Country for 30 years.

When on leave he found time to court and marry my grandmother, Ada Penny. His home was in Braemore, just across the Dorset border; hers was at Sixpenny Handley where, I understand, there are still many locals with the surname Penny.

When he finished his time with the Royal Navy he became a bread delivery man for Westons Bakers in Bournemouth – when bread, like milk, was delivered to the front door.

Because of his gait he was known as "Sailor". Small in stature, just five feet five inches and with a forward stoop, his feet

A Sailor's life for me

were permanently on the watch at ten-to-two with his hands usually clasped behind his back. My mother maintained that because of his stance she could spot a sailor from a mile away.

Washing Ahoy. . . and on high

Moving the family to Bournemouth, next to the sea as you would expect, Albert erected three huge posts – one in the front garden and two at the back – and from these were suspended cables and pulleys, not unlike the masts and rigging on a sailing ship. The rear system was utilised as a washing line. On windy days, when gathering in the washing, my petite grandmother often found herself suspended high in the air. Perhaps it was she who invented kite sailing back in the early '50s !

Probably at the insistence of the Local Authority, the time came for the removal of the pole and rigging from the front garden. I distinctly remember witnessing this as a young child.

Sailor roped in my father and uncle for this awkward task. They failed to realise the combined weight of pole and concrete base which duly 'brained' Uncle Frank, who had to be carried into the house where brandy was administered to revive him. He was never quite the same again !

Bread for the Dorset Nobs

Sailor's bread round was Talbot Woods, "amongst the Nobs" he would say. His customers knew he was a hoarder and would offer him all sorts of items rather than throw them away. He built up a fine silverware collection in this way. His car never saw the inside of his garage, as the space was too valuable and full of "usefuls", but my brothers and I did. We found it a place of wonders, particularly when finding a pistol and live ammunition! These were quickly disposed of down the well, never to be seen again.

Surviving in Dad's Army

At the start of the Second World War, grandfather joined the Home Guard. Not satisfied with having served King and Country for 30 years as a sailor, he became a soldier, with yet another uniform to clean!

The German Air Force chose to machine gun Bournemouth Town Centre when he was on his bread round. He survived by rolling under his delivery van but never said how many customers found bullets in their loaves of bread.

Sailor's customers had bullets not jam with their bread after a wartime Bournemouth Air Raid.
(A HOVIS advert from 1940)

Sailor, my grandfather, was very worldly wise. One piece of advice I remember was "never build on sand". I wonder what he would think of the property at the aptly named "Sandbanks" - currently the most expensive real estate outside London? How times have changed . . . !

Note: In 1939 many schoolchildren were evacuated from Portsmouth and Southampton to Bournemouth where, it was believed, they would be safe. But Bournemouth did not escape. During the Second World War well over 200 people were killed in German flying raids on the town.

Schooldays in Post-War Dorset

An appraisal of "then and now" by Dorsetman Professor Dennis Harding

WHEN I was a child in the nineteen-forties my grandfather had a remark which he would use to terminate any discussion that he felt was becoming too mentally taxing. With a sigh laden with experience and wisdom he would observe, "it will all be the same in the year 2000". How wrong he was, how utterly wrong! Not only has mankind polluted the environment to the point of irremediable damage, but after decades of political and social change, few traditional values in society remain unimpaired. Arrogance (self-assertiveness), avarice (wealth-creation) and selfish ambition (upward mobility) have replaced traditional virtues of humility and public service, touchy-feely self indulgence has replaced backbone and stiff upper lip of the kind grandad would have approved, and in almost every walk of life, including Higher Education, declining standards are camouflaged as improvements by the burgeoning new industry of Quality Assurance. Even for the Guides the individual 'self' has taken over from God and Country as the focus of allegiance. Contrary to his belief in the immutability of things, grandad would not have recognized the world in the year 2000, still less survived in it. In his day he would rather have gone bust than do anyone a dirty deal in business, and not surprisingly (since the world was changing already in those early post-war years), he did.

Grandad - Council-
lor Harry Best
(circa 1947)

Grandad would have been an anachronism in the twenty-first century. He believed in public service, and for a while was a much respected town councillor in Poole. I remember delivering canvassing leaflets for him with my mother in an early post-war election, but he eventually lost his seat because he refused to accept a party political ticket and independents eventually were driven out by the party machines. He is buried in a family plot at St Mary's, Longfleet, in the diocese of Salisbury, assuming that he has not been swept away in the tide of twenty-first century progress. That was what the local church proposed in 2007 in a planning application to build a new church hall over the graveyard, the existing hall over the road being deemed inadequate for the thriving happy-clappy congregation, and that site could presumably have been sold for other development to defray the costs. So the custodians of Christian values had decided that grandad could be moved aside in the name of progress. Grandad's team fortunately had several official war graves on its side, and after vigorous representations the application was withdrawn.

Born in Wartime

My recollections of the War itself are relatively few, and long since clouded by anecdotal repetition by my parents and their generation, who, in days when children were still supposed not to interrupt their elders and betters, did our recalling for us.

Poole was one of the ports that were regularly targeted by air raids, not so much as primary objectives, but where the bombers' payloads were dumped en route back to Germany when they had failed to make it to the industrial midlands. The ordnance factory on Holton Heath was certainly a target, and simulated buildings on Brownsea Island were used as a diversion. I certainly recall being dragged semi-somnolent to the Morrison shelter, or sometimes when the raids were particularly severe, being bedded down with my brother in the shelter all night. I also recall with a shudder being made to wear a gas-mask, its clammy rubber clasping my face tightly in its suffocating grasp. In the early hours of the morning my mother would cook breakfast for my grandad, who had been on ARP duty, and he would hand pieces of fried bread through the mesh of the shelter to us, running the gauntlet of my mother's stern exhortations to him not to do so.

My father was away in the RAF, having volunteered before conscription, correctly anticipating thereby that he might get the choice of a better billet. When he returned on leave I was allowed to stay up to meet the train, and he then had the wearisome task of carrying me on the long walk home on his shoulders. Like all small boys, we idolized the aces of the air, and none more than 'Cat's Eyes' Cunningham and his fellow night fighter pilots, whose fabled diet of carrots supposedly enabled them to see the enemy in the dark. Years later the only time I ever remember my father showing any anxiety at my own flying was when one of my friends misguidedly told him that I was taking a night rating; it took long and patient persuasion to convince him that we had runway lights in place of goose-neck flares, and that my undercarriage was in no danger of failing to deploy through battle damage.

Shortly after the War ended I remember him taking me to his old aerodrome, where I heard for the first time the truly awesome sound of the jet engine of a Gloster Meteor whining up to full power in a hangar. I must have been six or seven at the time, and found the concept of an aeroplane without a propeller still hard to grasp, even though they had been in service already in the later years of the War. I suppose my interest in flying stemmed from this background, though I never had the slightest desire to join the service nor even to fly aerobatically. For me, flying was solely a means of achieving an archaeological objective, though I must confess that a good landing in adverse weather conditions- not always realized in practice it should be said- added to the sense of achievement.

For the first five years of my life I had known no state other than War, and I found my parents' reminiscences about what they had done 'before the War', the holidays they had enjoyed and the theatres or restaurants that they had frequented about as unreal and remote as tales of King Arthur or classical history. Their reassurances, countering any childhood tantrum, that 'after the War' one would be able to have toys that were not broken hand-me-downs and taste strange foodstuffs like bananas proved in the event to be something of an anticlimax, as the country embarked upon five years of post-war austerity. One thought that haunted me as a child was what I would be required to do in the next war. Simple arithmetic told me that if the peace between my grandfather's and father's war was any indication, then I should be involved in the next by my late twenties. There were still plenty of reminders of the relatively recent Great War, like the decorator that my parents usually employed to paint the house, whom we were told politely to ignore as he muttered and twitched at the top of his ladder, an affliction attributed to gassing or shell-shock in the trenches.

Given that there had never been two major wars that had so comprehensively affected every family in the land, I could never understand in later life why in the aftermath of Hitler's War that there was such a spate of films that glamorized the whole dreadful business, or more particularly why a population that had rejected so comprehensively the architect of victory in the 1945 'Khaki' General Election should wish to pay at the box office to see them.

. . . . and so to School

I went to junior school just as the War was ending. I have clear memories of the Headmaster, a slightly-built Scot who had been an officer in the Royal Navy, and who imposed his military regime upon us five to eleven-year olds in a manner which would have flattered the Hitlerjugend. We wore grey flannel uniforms with a black and white striped tie and a badge with the monogram emblazoned on the breast pocket of our jackets, on top of which a (navy) blue gabardine raincoat was regulation dress. On arrival each day and after mid-morning or lunch-time breaks a whistle signalled the bedlam of activity in the playground to stop, and we stood, frozen like a still frame within a movie sequence, until a second whistle commanded us to line up in serried ranks by 'house', denoted by the colours red, yellow, green and blue. Head of each rank was the 'house captain', except for the rank whose captain was duty monitor that week, whose task was to hold open the door and ensure that no mischief took place in the cloakroom. At a given signal, each rank marched off, in step and with arms swinging to the horizontal, saluting both duty master and duty monitor (the navy salute, not the army, of course) en route to the cloakroom. The school had an excellent academic record, with an impressive success rate in the 11-plus. It also excelled in sport, and in the annual borough school sports invariably carried off most of the prizes; I still have half a dozen of the little brass medals that were the cherished reward for out-running or out-jumping the Unterkinder from other establishments. At the beginning of the proceedings we marched past, impeccably turned out in white vests and black shorts, our marching attracting admiration from a generation of parents who believed in discipline, smart kit and short-back-and-sides. I was about to say that it never did us any harm, and may even have done us some good, but I realize that I am the last to be able to make such a judgement. I can therefore only say that I bear no physical scars, and my memories are largely happy ones. Whether others less agile in sport or less able academically would share that view is another matter.

Poole Grammar School

One of my class teachers at junior school who made a particular impression was a spinster lady who could easily have been a role model for Margaret Rutherford, having the same full-bosomed figure and multiple chins, the only difference being that she balanced her pince-nez on a beak-like nose which earned her the nickname 'Polly'. She believed in the importance of spelling, learning tables by rote, and could not abide grubby necks or dirty finger-nails. Cleanliness was next to godliness, we should waste not nor want not, or whatnot; I cannot recall all the homespun philosophy. But it all led to our school textbooks being carefully wrapped in brown paper covers, and Friday afternoons being devoted to polishing our desk-tops until they shone, however deeply scored with the initials of earlier generations or stained with ink spilled from the wells, which seemed to upset from their sockets without the slightest provocation.

Merit was rewarded with a red star, malfeasance with a black, the whole tally being recorded on a massive board in the corridor where every pupil's name was listed by 'house'. I cannot now remember what it all led to at the end of the session, which suggests that it was hardly a traumatic denouement.

Growing up

My memories of senior school are surprisingly few, having been obliterated almost as comprehensively as the buildings themselves that were swept away in a phase of urban re-development in the 1960s. My first year coincided with the Festival of Britain in 1951, when senior pupils, including my older brother, were taken to London to see the Skylon and other attractions first hand, while we juniors were merely permitted a totally unmemorable half-day event locally. A year later I recall a real sense of shock and grief at being summoned en masse to the school hall one frosty February morning to be told that the king had died. Even as a child the twin presences of Churchill and the king, the one revered as our wartime hero, the other familiar from his Christmas broadcasts, to which the family invariably listened, gathered around the wireless at three o'clock after Christmas dinner. When George VI in 1939 had given his 'man at the gate of the year' speech it genuinely struck a chord across the nation that made more recent Christmas speeches seem superficial and formulaic. I remember that morning we sang a rousing rendition of 'For all the saints who from their labour rest'. Within a few months the national spirit revived to embrace the idea of a new Elizabethan age, epitomized in the Coronation of 1953. By this time we were clustered, not round the wireless, but around a flickering, snowy, nine-inch television, admiring the state coaches and processions, and especially the large and irrepressibly cheerful figure of Queen Salote of Tonga, braving the weather in an open-topped carriage. By the middle of the decade the Goons on radio declared 'it's good to be alive in 1955'

Poole Grammar School

and a couple of years later Harold MacMillan was assuring us that we had never had it so good.

The 1950s was also a decade in which science was seen as the key to a brighter future. My brother had been outstandingly good at physics and chemistry, achieving numerous prizes and progressing to university forthwith, having deferred his National Service. Science was regarded with a faith and confidence that now seems culpably naïve as the answer to all life's ills, and anyone of academic promise needed great determination to resist the school's coercion towards specialization in science. I by contrast preferred English and History, and was a great disappointment to the science staff, one of whom wrote despairingly on my report 'Position, 32/32: he seems not to be interested, but spends long periods staring out of the window…'. Progressing to the Arts Sixth Form, I added Latin to make my trio of subjects, in which I eventually achieved a very modest pass to accompany my rather better results in the two major subjects. Regarding my Latin master's congratulations as a trifle over the top, I protested modestly that my grade did me little credit. 'No matter, my boy', he insisted, 'the important thing is that we shall never have to suffer this mutual misery again!' He added presciently that I would never be without my Latin, a remark that I have often had occasion to reflect upon in later life.

Apart from Physics, academically I progressed with reasonable success, particularly in History and English. My history teacher was a delightful man but hopeless idealist, who believed in the socialist utopia and was a leading light in the Esperanto movement. At the same time he was nostalgic about his Oxford days that seemed to have been dedicated to liberal intellectualism and good claret. My English teacher, a graduate of St John's at Cambridge, where he had been influenced by F. R. Leavis, had been a major in his twenties in the war against the Japanese, suffering severe ill health for several years in consequence. He was unlike the other ex-officers on the staff, who paraded their moustaches and exploits with great bravado. He simply didn't talk about it, but effortlessly commanded the respect of the school. I owe both a great debt for setting me on the road to higher education. But I wish that the History Man had not been so insistent that I should read History, and that his English colleague had not simply and perhaps shrewdly been content to leave the decision to me, because that way I might have read History, to which I was better suited, instead of English, which I chose simply to assert my teenage independence.

Animal, Vegetable or Mineral? v Time Team

It was at school that I first became involved in archaeology. The school Archaeological Society had previously excavated a Romano-British kiln site at Ower, on the southern shore of Poole harbour, before moving to a longer-term project at Studland. My brother, who was five years older than me, had been one of the team of senior boys involved, so I was tolerated and allowed to go through the spoil heaps for finds that others might have missed, a task that was not nearly as unproductive as it should have been.   When he left, I stuck with it, spending many weekends acquiring dexterity with the trademark trowel. The site was a Romano-British farmstead not far from Ballard Down, where I spent many happy weekends cycling, walking and digging during my teenage schooldays.   The hum of dragonflies, the dancing of butterflies on the chalk downs that led to Old Harry Rocks and the excitement of the occasional adder in the heath-lands was combined with the thrill of discovery on excavating a sherd of Iron Age pottery or the base of a Samian platter impressed with the name of its potter.   I have happy memories of cycling to Sandbanks, trying to avoid the ticket inspector on the crossing by chain-ferry to Shell Bay, and then free-wheeling down the hill on the way back and waving at the toll kiosk as we sped by, hoping to salvage an unspent ticket for use the following weekend.   My early start in archaeology was by no means unique, and I believe that several professors of my generation began their careers this way.

I suppose at that time every schoolboy was an aspiring archaeologist, prompted by the virtuoso performances of Sir Mortimer Wheeler on the television parlour show, Animal, Vegetable, Mineral?   It is interesting to compare the TV stereotypes of the 1950s with the stereotypes parodied on the recent Time Team version of popular archaeology. AVM had the military type in Wheeler, ex-brigadier in the Eighth Army and a self-promoting successor to General Pitt-Rivers. In fact he was a survivor of a unique generation, having served as a subaltern at Passchendaele and as an artillery commander at El Alamein, either one of which would have been more than enough for most mortals.   Chairman of the panel and its question-master was the suave bow-tied Cambridge don of good taste and manners, Glyn Daniel, an authority on chambered tombs of the Neolithic and later Disney Professor of Archaeology at Cambridge.

Among other regulars was the archetypal nutty professor in Gordon Childe, who by then had moved from the Abercromby Chair at Edinburgh that I was later to occupy to the London Institute of Archaeology that Wheeler had founded.

In the more recent series, the donnish type in bow tie survived, but the nutty professor was replaced by the scruffy professor, whose garish threadbare jumper and unkempt hair proclaimed him to be a great intellectual. Nowadays, of course, the team had to include the obligatory Regional Accent, in this case an exaggerated version of a character from The Archers, though a Scouser or Geordie would have done as well.   Time Team also included the mandatory woman, as it happens the only one who came across as truly sane and professional.   Like the weather forecast, modern broadcasting has dumbed down the Reith-inspired belief that the purpose of television is to inform as well as to entertain, and seemingly disregards the possibility that viewers might be just as intelligent as the presenters.

Leaving School

The episode that soured my departure from the school, however, was not related to archaeology or my scholastic performance, but to my taking French leave on the occasion of the annual school sports, when I should have been conspicuously in evidence rallying the chaps. My brother, now graduated and employed by the Atomic Energy Authority (during which time he had been one of the first drafted in to counter the meltdown crisis in 1957 at the Windscale reactor, now known as Sellafield), was about to emigrate to Australia, where he had obtained a position with their Atomic Energy Commission. There was some urgency, since his exemption from National Service expired once he had given notice to the UKEAE, so we arranged to meet at short notice. I had hoped that my unauthorized absence might pass unremarked, but unfortunately and coincidentally, a couple of my fellow House Captains had failed to enter into the spirit of the games, and had taken an afternoon's sailing on the harbour, leading the authorities to assume that we had all been together. Our absence was indeed noted and, as the jargon of the cinema screens at the time might have had it, the balloon went up good and proper, and no mistake. With hindsight it all seems very trivial, but at the time it appeared to put our careers in terminal jeopardy.

It was therefore some relief on arrival at college in Oxford to find that others had enjoyed a rather more chequered school career than mine, and far from jeopardizing my future, the episode seemed to be regarded by dons as the one indication of initiative in what otherwise was evidently considered to be a thoroughly predictable school track record. What I did not know at the time was that I would never return to live in Dorset, and that, by the time I made a return visit, my childhood haunts would have long since succumbed to progress. Grandad would certainly no longer have recognized the town he knew and served.

Editor's note:

Professor Dennis William Harding MA DPhil FRSE, a Life Member of the Society, wrote the acclaimed autobiographical feature in the 2014 Year Book on his early 1960s archaeological dig at Pimperne while an undergraduate at Keble College, Oxford.

He went on to become a Senior Lecturer at Durham University and then to Edinburgh where he held the Abercromby Chair of Prehistoric Archaeology for thirty years from 1977 to 2007.

He is the author of the 2012 Iron Age Hillforts in Britain and Beyond – an impressive work of great worth and interest to students and scholars of prehistory and archaeology as well as those of heritage and environmental studies.

Other acclaimed books include The Archaeology of Celtic Art (2007) and The Iron Age Round-house (2009).

Café on The Cliff - Boscombe's best kept little Secret!

Leslie Allard waxes lyrical on a favourite place

A cup of Dorset Tea and a slice of Dorset Apple Cake made to Chef's speciality recipe - an indulgence, a treat, or may-be just irresistible, any excuse will do!

View to the Isle of Wight

On a hot summer's day, here before my eyes are scrumptious gastronomical delights, strategically placed to tease, tempt and catch both the intentional and impulse purchase. Well - we all have our weaknesses. If not sweet toothed there are plenty of savoury choices. Toasted tea cakes, a variety of sandwiches/baguettes and hot 'toasties' complete with salad and chips - a range of jacket potatoes and omelettes with different mouth-watering fillings, full English or other breakfast combinations, maybe something exotic like deep fried calamari with chips, sweet chilli dip and salad. On Sunday ' A Traditional Sunday Lunch' with a choice of two roast meats, roast potatoes, a medley of fresh seasonal vegetables, Yorkshire pudding and a rich red wine gravy and a choice of two old fashioned puddings - one hot, one cold!' - or perhaps just enjoy an Ice-Cream! That was all my daughter wanted as we came up from the beach and she read the sign-board. That's what took us in. We were hooked.

Sitting on the terrace enjoying afternoon tea and a game of bowls, on 'the green' below, is quiet and tranquil and as quintessentially English as a village cricket match, although neither rural or town centre but by the sea, on a cliff top. This is Boscombe Overcliff with beautiful panoramic coastal views from the Isle of Wight to the Purbecks. "Café on The Cliff" -it says in small-print -is Boscombe's "Best Kept Little Secret". Well it was up to now any-way!

The Café is situated within The club house of Boscombe Cliff Bowling Club, established 1904. The bowlers enjoy their teas! - like Wimbledon and strawberries, Henley and a picnic with Pimms, or a Grand Prix and champagne.   However this is not exclusively for the bowlers, it's open to the public. Entry is like walking into a 'time-machine'. Even when built, circa 1927, the design of the attractive pavilion harked back to 'elegant Edwardian England'. Now it's a quiet haven, providing an escape from the hustle & bustle of today's fast-paced modern life.

Boscombe Cliff Bowls

The club house is full of nostalgia. Proudly on display are artefacts and memorabilia - magnificent wooden boards cover the walls almost entirely. They, like the rolls of war-time remembrance, carry names and dates but of the clubs presidents, winners of matches and tournaments, both of the past and the present. These together with the respective trophies, photographs and press cuttings all capture the memorable moments that bring to life all the achievements which have been and are happening here on this green.

Proprietor Paul

Paul, the proprietor of the Cafe, is by no means Edwardian, nor "stiff and starchy" but he is very English - with a capital E!   He proudly enjoys promoting all things typically English   in   his   establishment. Hence his menu containing old classics, like bread pudding, flap jacks, rock cakes and cream teas. Relaxed and good humoured with a natural un-assuming manner Paul makes customers feel part of the establishment.

The word Cafe is perhaps an injustice, as this is in a league well beyond and above a pre-conceived idea of the ubiquitous greasy spoon. The subtleties, like flowers on tables, and in the toilets too, and 'art-deco style' menu cards and the main display board, all add to the charm of this quaint place. The venue could be the setting for an Agatha Christie's drama. Although there is no canned music, in my mind I can hear the Charleston being played on a Gramophone and imagine society ladies and trendy 'flappers' dancing.

How did Paul come to be here? "The place was in decline," he said. "My father, a Club member, was asked if he thought I would be interested in it, so by a sort of invitation, here I am! It's now surpassed the Club's expectations." Paul's not a 'faceless' manager, not haughty or full of self-importance, just quietly 'getting on with it,' making a living. He tells me that he works hard for six months of the year and has six months off. Soon to be starting his tenth year, "in one of the best locations in the country - it is after-all, where people come to enjoy a holiday!"- he added " It's pleasing for me to give something back to the community. I'm happy here, I live nearby, I walk to work every-day. I like Bournemouth, its home, it's were I grew up. I just want to maintain the status quo and eventually pass on the ethos of this place, the community spirit, to someone who is like-minded". He is a humble and modest man who learnt his skills in the "University of Life". His parents moved to Bournemouth in 1968, in the hotel trade. His Father switched from golf to bowls which led to his

Across the piers

mother, together with Paul, helping behind the scenes in the Bowling Club's Café. Paul grew up playing and developing a knowledge of bowls. Perhaps his affiliation with the place introduced him to the catering profession in which he was to pursue a successful career. A Royal Marines Boy Soldier from the age of 16 at 18 he decided the forces were not for him. He wanted to be in the catering world, in "Front of

House". Whilst working at a hotel he studied at college, progressed to the Royal Bath in Bournemouth, then "The Liners."

During his time with the Queen Elizabeth 2 -as a silver-service head waiter - the liner was pressed into service to support the task force at the time of the Falklands War. Ironically for someone who decided not to pursue the Royal Marines he was awarded the South Atlantic Medal for his services whilst on board having served in the 'theatre of operations.' A colleague at the time was, years later, arrested, tried and convicted, for five murders, becoming known as the Ipswich Strangler.

He moved on again, and "jumped ship" to the Oriana, operating out of Sydney Australia, and providing cruises to the south pacific islands. After three years it was time to move on again, this time returning to the UK and home to Bournemouth. After a short well earned rest Australia beckoned so he set off with a "working Visa" touring and working around Australia, actually deciding to emigrate in the 1990's when procuring a job with the Western Australia Cricket Association as their food and beverages manager, which he enjoyed for ten years.

The U.K. called and so it was back home to Bournemouth once again. . . and the Café on the Cliff. Open from 09:00 - 5:30 seven days a week from Easter - October, he and his staff of long-standing will be there to welcome you.

Free car-parking abounds in the area too. There's cliff top walks, the beach, a game or 'play' at bowls - (as mentioned previously it's open to the public so anybody can hire the woods for a nominal charge and have a go!) There's something for everyone. It's a real Dorset Gem. So go and enjoy the experience! (Café on the Cliff, Boscombe Cliff Bowling Club, Woodland Avenue Boscombe BH5 2DJ).

THE COLLITON CLUB - Dorchester

The Colliton Club has been in existence for over 60 years. It is a registered private company limited by guarantee, and operates as a members' social club. Applications for membership are always welcome. Associate membership is £10 per annum.

The Club caters for breakfast, lunches and evening meals, using locally sourced food wherever possible with a selection of hot and cold drinks.

The Club has 2 skittle alleys, dart boards, snooker and pool tables and a table tennis room. There is also a club golf society.

Rooms are available to hire (evenings only) for private functions such as birthdays, anniversaries, and weddings. Priority is always given to club members.

Frank Palmer

Memories of life in the Blackmore Vale

An appraisal from a recently published autobiography   by Philip Knott

FRANK Palmer was born in 1915 in the gamekeeper's cottage in Up Cerne Wood near Cerne Abbas. His father Ernest Palmer was working alongside Frank's grandfather George Foot, who was employed as woodman on the Up Cerne Manor Estate. Shortly after Frank was born his parents moved to Hamworthy where his father worked in an ammunition factory, manufacturing armaments for the war effort. At the age of two his mother contracted tuberculosis, an illness that was to claim her life before he was old enough to even remember her, one of his greatest regrets.

Frank Palmer- a true Dorset countryman

AFTER the First World War his father took up employment as a gardener at East Coker Manor near Yeovil, living in one of a pair of estate cottages, now submerged under Sutton Bingham Reservoir.

The early years

In 1920 his father started work as a farm labourer at Manor Farm at Stourton Caundle. Mr Douch had recently purchased the farm from the Stourhead Estate, at the final dispersal sale of land and property, owned by Sir Henry Hoare of Stourhead, in the parishes of Stourton and Purse Caundle.

Local School's infant class in 1920 with Frank in the centre of the front row

Frank attended the village primary school and was the last pupil to complete his entire education at the school, recalling in his memoirs: "My hand would shoot up into the air every time that a question was asked, even though I rarely knew the answer. This ploy was always worth a try, for the tendency was for those who had not put up their hands to be asked. Of course there were occasions when this course of action backfired, although I always had some sort of answer ready, even if it was nearly always incorrect. The most unwelcome visitor to the school was the Police Constable from Stalbridge. I was full of apprehension as he came through the door and would cast my mind back, to recall any recent mischief that I had been involved with, which he might be about to investigate. On the occasions when it turned out that he was only on a social visit there would be a huge sigh of relief from the boy pupils present."

General learning and corporal punishment

" Punishment was a subject that I was aware of, starting from my early school days. The first smack, for both my brother and myself, was for rolling around on the unmade surface of the school yard. The surface consisted of loose gravel and dust, so it is not difficult to imagine just how dirty we both became. I used to observe how different pupils reacted to chastisement. There were some pupils, like my brother and myself, who became hardened to it. There were some who would show great determination, to ensure that they were not seen to be shedding a tear, although their bottom lip could be seen to quiver, as they fought to keep back the tears. They also tended to sulk for a period after receiving their punishment. There were others of course, who would start to cry, before the cane had even reached the palm of their hand. On several occasions irate parents of children came to the school door to complain about the punishment their child had received. They received little time or sympathy and were soon sent on their way by the Head Teacher. One teacher offered pupils a choice of punishment, not that it was of any consolation to the pupil concerned. Her preferred forms of punishment were to either send a child to stand in the corner, with a book placed on their head, or to write lines after school hours. If a pupil found the boredom of writing lines or the indignity of standing in the corner too much to bear, then she would give pupils the choice of the quick option, which was of course the cane. If a pupil chose the cane, the head teacher then asked the child to fetch the cane from the cupboard."

No fun on the farm

At the age of ten, Frank was hand milking four cows before and after school each day. In his memoirs Frank recalled "When it was first suggested to me that it was time for me to start hand milking at Manor Farm, I initially felt that this was a good idea, considering myself to be growing up, and becoming a young man. The novelty did not last long however. I soon found out that there is no enjoyment in having to get up at 6 o'clock every morning, especially during wintertime, having to exchange a nice warm bed for a freezing cold cow stall. I also became disenchanted with the fact that I had

Manor Farm at Stourton Caundle

to run home straight after school, change into my old clothes, and go milking, while other boys were allowed out to play. In the mornings I rushed home after milking for breakfast and a quick wash, probably better described as a cat's lick. I then changed into my school clothes, followed by a short scamper up the street, to arrive at school just in the nick of time. My wage was one shilling and sixpence a week, for working both morning and afternoon milking, seven days a week. The money was paid to my father and used to help provide food and clothing for the family."

Nothing to sing about

Frank was a member of St Peter's Church Choir, recalling in his memoirs: "Before joining the church choir I was forced to attend the Sunday morning church service and the evening service at the chapel. As a member of the church choir I had to wear the same heavy hob nailed boots on Sundays that I wore during the rest of the week. These boots had to be dry on Saturday night, so that they would polish up sparkling and bright for the Sunday morning service and woe betide me if they did not.

As regards to the choir's singing I am afraid that the old adage 'practice makes perfect' did not apply in our case. I suppose our enthusiasm made up for what we lacked in finesse. This religious commitment continued for over two years, though I doubt if I could have claimed the credit for my excellent record of attendance, as this was entirely due to the insistence of my stepmother. Every Thursday evening the choir would assemble in the church and we composed ourselves in readiness for the start of yet another monotonous choir practice. It really must have been doubtful as to whether these weekly sessions ever helped us to attain a higher standard, by singing the correct words of any given hymn, psalm or anthem in tune. It would have been fair comment if someone had described me as being in the choir for the sole purpose of making up the numbers, although I am pretty sure I would have been given full marks for both good behaviour and my willingness to improve on my singing. Only once did I receive a payment for being such an untalented chorister, when I received a half a crown from the bridegroom. I suppose it was a reward for having appeared to look somewhat angelic throughout the marriage ceremony.

A planned visit by the Bishop of Salisbury had meant many hours of extra rehearsal for the regular members of the church choir. The service was quite an impressive affair for the blessing of Mr George Fernandes, who resided at Haddon Lodge, to become a lay reader. Everyone in the choir and a few members of the congregation were to gather at the church gates to watch the Bishop taking his final leave, bidding farewell to Reverend Fincher and several other church dignitaries. The Bishop was about to step into his chauffeur driven car, when he commented on the choir, comparing the quality of our singing with that of skylarks. I have a suspicion that he was showing a lot of tact when speaking so highly of our singing ability. One person within earshot took a somewhat cynical view of such praise and afterwards was heard to compare our singing with that of a nest of cawing rooks".

Village outings

From the age of five Frank went on every annual village outing, recalling in his memoirs: "until the mid 1920s the annual village outing to the seaside started from the front of the school, where we climbed excitedly aboard the farm wagons and sat on bundles of clean straw. It was then a journey of three miles to the railway station at Stalbridge to wait impatiently for the steam train to arrive, followed by a mad scramble to climb up into a railway carriage to claim a seat by a window.

From the middle of the 1920s a fleet of charabancs were hired from a Mr Seager of Sherborne. The children would take a few coppers to school during the course of the year, for the Headmistress to hold in safekeeping for them as spending money for the annual outing. The children would also help to raise money for their fares, by taking part in a Christmas Concert held in the Hut. The young men of the village would also contribute the collection from their Good Friday football match held in Meslams Field between the married and single men of the village.

We climbed excitedly aboard one of the three the charabancs, parked outside the Trooper Inn, and settled into a wooden bench seat bolted to the floor of the vehicle, hoping the weather would remain dry for the entire journey to Weymouth, with the canvass hood rolled down. Our next door neighbour shared the responsibility with my step mother, keeping an eye on both sets of children as we played on the sand, taking

Ready for the off - Village outing in the mid 1920s

it in turns to accompany each child when fetching a bucketful of water from the sea. A man on the beach sculpted famous buildings from the wet sand and passers-by threw coins from the promenade, in appreciation of his artistic attributes. A picnic lunch prepared by my stepmother provided a plenteous supply of food and drink, grains of sand grated against my teeth when munching away at a sandwich. Our pocket money would not last all day. A visit to the Woolworths store was a great attraction, while the Punch and Judy show kept us amused on the beach. There was a four-wheeled carriage, pulled by a goat, giving children a ride along the promenade. The cost of an ice cream and for a ride on a donkey were the only treats that myself and my brother could realistically expect to receive

Trooper Inn and Bridge Cottages at Stourton Caundle

Free afternoon teas were provided for all of the children in a restaurant in the town, thanks to the generosity of the Fernandes family from Haddon Lodge, who travelled to Weymouth to meet the villagers and organise the seating arrangements. This was one of a number of occasions when the Fernandes family most generously gave both their time and money to the children of Stourton Caundle. A child carrying a bucketful of sand in one hand, and clutching a little wooden spade in the other, was a familiar sight at the start of the journey home. The womenfolk went in search of a piece of seaweed to use as a barometer for the next twelve months.

Rowdy and ribald return home

Stopping to gaze up at the Cerne Giant would invariably bring out the worst in one or two of the women present. One could not fail but to hear some of their ribald remarks about his attributes. There was a stop off at a public house, with some of the adults volunteering to keep the children under control, while the remainder went into the pub. Some of the women, who would not be seen in either Gwyers Ale House or the Trooper Inn, were determined to let their hair down for once, without any concern for what others might say, as they downed a glass or two of stout with gay abandon. This was the only occasion, during the course of the whole year, when the men and women present were able to escape from the harshness of every day working life, for just a few short hours".

On leaving school at the age of thirteen Frank took up full time employment at Manor Farm working seven days a week looking after the pigs.

Music then disappointment and tragedy

Shortly before the outbreak of the Second World War, he joined the Dorset County Council Highways Department working as a roadman, which meant that he had Saturday afternoons and Sundays off.

With the outbreak of the war, Frank, like his father before him, failed a medical for the armed forces. He was assigned to a number of jobs during the war years, including spells at the Okeford Fitzpaine dairy, making butter and cheese and as a member of the ground staff at the Royal Naval Air Station, HMS Dipper at Henstridge.

During the mid 1930s Frank taught himself to play the saxophone and clarinet, and joined the village brass band, taking part in the procession through the village for the Coronation of King George VI. He also joined a local dance band known as the Bing Boys, performing in village halls around the Blackmore Vale. He became a very proficient musician, and later made many guest appearances with dance bands made up from American troops stationed at Gibbs Marsh Stalbridge.

His playing career was to finish on a sad note at the end of the War, following news of the death of his stepbrother Stanley at the hands of the Japanese while a prisoner of war working on the infamous Burma Siam Railway. Stanley was his soul mate and they had been inseparable throughout their formative years, into all sorts of mischief and a cause of constant concern to their parents. The sad loss of his stepbrother was a tragedy for Frank and he never picked up a musical instrument again.

During the war Frank was a member of the Lydlinch Platoon of the Home Guard.

Back on the road

At the end of the war Frank returned to work for the Dorset County Council Highways Department. In 1954 was promoted to the position of road roller driver, a job he held for the next 25 years.

Frank was a fiercely independent man, and did not want to be a burden to anyone. He consistently refused all offers of help until just before the end. He was by nature in adult life a shy person yet in later life he would talk non-stop for hours, recalling memories from his childhood in his wonderful Dorset accent.

Frank Palmer with his trusty typewriter

Following his retirement in 1979 Frank purchased a typewriter, and became a prolific writer, aided by an incredible memory he could recall incidents from seventy or more years ago in the greatest of detail. Frank was a true Dorset man and a true countryman.

His memories as recorded in a recently published book entitled 'Memories of Life in a Blackmore Vale Village' provide the reader with an insight into the harshness of everyday life for rural working class families, during the 1920s and 1930s. The book highlights the magnitude of the changes in village life since the end of the Second World War and will provide a valuable social and historical record for future generations of Dorset residents. Memories of Life in a Blackmore Vale Village is published by Natula Publications Christchurch with a retail price of £6-95p.

The Dorsets
- turning the tide of war in India

The story of their role at the Battle of
Kohima by Rev. Dr. John Travell

> When you go home
> Tell them of us: and say
> For their tomorrow
> We gave our today.

THESE words, known as the Kohima Epitaph, spoken at every war memorial remembrance event, are engraved on a monument in the remote Naga Hills, on the borders of Burma, India and Assam. They commemorate the great battle of Kohima – enormously important in turning the war in the far east against Japan. After it the Japanese forces were in retreat and secured no further significant victories.

In his History of the Second World War, Winston Churchill wrote that "the valiant defence of Kohima against enormous odds was a fine episode".

Churchill's brief account of the battle makes no mention of the role of the 2nd Battalion of the Dorset Regiment who played an heroic and decisive part in the defeat of the Japanese.

In January 1944 the Japanese launched a pre-emptive attack to prevent the British and Indian armies from an offensive to re-take Burma. Some 13,500 Japanese soldiers were directed to stop reinforcements coming to the aid of the British at Imphal but, to do this, they needed to overcome the small garrison on the Kohima ridge which blocked their passage on the road to India.

On this small British hill station was a field bakery, a hospital, a leave camp and a battle casualty reinforcement camp. As the administrative centre for Nagaland, there was also the British Commissioner's bungalow, a club house and tennis court. Occupying this area were about 1,500 combatant troops together with soldiers who were on leave or convalescent.

The Japanese attack began on 4 April 1944. The steep sided and heavily forested ridge was formed with seven hill positions – the last defensive position being the bungalow and tennis court.

Supported by an artillery bombardment, the Japanese steadily advanced towards the fiercely defended tennis court and captured the vital water supply. Luckily for the garrison, a small spring was discovered which, however, could only be reached at night.

To relieve the desperate situation, the British 2nd Division, which was 2000 miles away in south west India, was rushed by every means of road, rail and air transport, to help the besieged garrison. The Brigade which included the 2nd Battalion of the Dorset Regiment met and defeated elements of the enemy at Zuba, 15 miles north of Kohima. The attack on the Japanese at Kohima, with air, artillery and armour support, was launched on 18 April – just hours after the Commissioner's bungalow was captured and destroyed.

The tennis court became the field of battle; with the combatants in trenches just 50 yards apart it was close enough to be fought with hand grenades.

While fierce fighting continued – often hand-to-hand – on other areas of the ridge, the British 6th Brigade was able to take over from the original garrison defenders who had withheld the siege against overwhelming odds for over two weeks. It was now 20 April.

Fighting continued along the whole ridge with the Japanese putting up a fierce resistance and at the tennis court the battle continued to rage. Victory was vital in order to reopen the road for support tanks to be brought up and free the way through to Imphal.

The 2nd Battalion Dorsets Memorial at Kohima

On 13 May the 2nd Battalion, the Dorset Regiment, was able to capture the area of the bungalow and finally clear the tennis court and the whole of the Kohima ridge.

With the road reopened and in the height of the monsoon season the campaign continued for another six weeks forcing the Japanese to retreat until 22 June when the British 2nd Division met up with the 5th Indian Infantry Division, 30 miles south of Kohima

Returning to Kohima, the Dorsets built a battallion memorial on the tennis courts to those who had been killed where the hardest fighting had been. The wording on the memorial plaque includes the motto of the Society of Dorset Men which they had proudly adopted.

> In Memory of All Ranks of
> The 2nd Battalion of the
> Dorsetshire Regt.
> Who fell in action
> In these hills between
> April-June 1944
> Who's afeard.

After a period of rest and recovery, the Dorsets then rejoined their Brigade and led the way back through Burma pursuing the Japanese until April 1945 when they were taken out by air.

To mark the 70th anniversary

A clarion call – clear and shrill and haunting – broke the still morning silence of the sleepy village of Charminster, near Dorchester.

Trumpeter with the Durnovarian Silver Band, Mrs. Anne Jones, was playing the Last Post after her husband, the Rev. Peter Jones, had conducted a short but moving "Kohima" service of remembrance at the War Memorial in the churchyard of St. Mary's.

A floral tribute was laid on the Memorial by Paul Snow,
on behalf of the Society of Dorset Men..

Attending the Kohima Memorial were: (from the left) - Cllr. Peter Mann (Mayor of Dorchester), Keith Russell and Keith Wilson(formerly of the Royal Signals), Adrian Downton (whose uncle Sgt.Maj. Herbert Downton died fighting hand-to-hand on the tennis court at Kohima), Rev. Dr. John Travell and Trevor Vacher-Dean (Committeemen of The Society of Dorset Men), Rev. Peter Jones, Max Loder and Trudy Ritsema (representing St. Mary's School), 'Bob' Manning (who was born in Dorchester Barracks and arrived at Kohima in Sept. 1945 to 'mop up' after the Japanese defeat), Beverly Lenthall (who produced the floral tribute) and trumpeter Anne Jones.

A Himalayan Oddysey

Dorset youngsters have an adventure   *by John Hegarty*

Setting: The Tibetan Plateau of Kashmir

ON the second day of mountain biking, moving towards the monastery at Hemis, our supporting drivers were unwilling to take their vehicles up the last few miles of track judging it too rough. Rather than ride on unsupported, it was decided to camp at Nimo. This was a sleepy Himalayan village where the local teacher allowed us to camp in an apricot grove which surrounds his house. The location was ideal and approximately 300m above the Indus River which cuts through the valley below. His house was over 200 years old and his land had never been hit by the elements.

Previous nights had been clear and star-filled but on this evening a storm started to rumble in from the adjacent valley. The youngsters were in their tents sleeping. The storm intensified and it was clear that this was going to be something special. The thunder became one continuous roar and frequent lightning bolts raged around us. Rainfall was incredibly heavy but this presented no obvious problem. The area was so elevated, surface water disappeared rapidly.

Picturing the disaster

Unfortunately high above us, an unseen mountain stream in an adjacent valley had been blocked, probably by a landslide, and behind this dam a huge lake was forming.

Suddenly the ground began to shake as in an earthquake. The dam far above us gave way and a 35ft high wall of mud and rocks swept down the mountainside.

This altered direction towards us and missed our tents by approximately 15m. It devastated forests, houses, embankments and virtually everything in its path. Nothing was spared. Steel bridges were smashed as if matchwood and trucks moving on the road to Leh were carried down into the Indus River and swept away. The storm continued to rage and in the darkness it was not clear what had happened but the stream bed alongside our campsite was now a deep gorge and the adjacent land was covered in a thick glutinous mud. With first light it became obvious that the local area had been devastated and that we were trapped. The road through the village was cut on both sides of us giving no possibility of escape.

We decided to move camp into the village because, although much lower in the valley, it offered greater forestry protection. We ended up relocating the entire group by ladder to the roof of the 'mud-hut' village bank, ten feet above the ground.

The following day the army started looking for missing soldiers from a nearby base and frequent helicopters were seen searching the riverbed and valley. One sepoy was found alive but others, along with the truck drivers, were killed.

More storms and landslides

The day remained bright but at sunset the same pattern of storms descended upon us. A guard rota was in place and at around midnight the first landslide hit just to the west of us wiping out another part of the army camp and killing three more soldiers. Our group huddled in a torrential downpour as a smaller landslide kicked off to the west. Sitting together with locals in the pouring rain we awaited the next landslide. The storm soon abated and we returned to our campsite to sleep in full clothing with tents left open to allow for a fast evacuation.

Another bright day dawned but there was no movement along the highway and no attempts to bridge the stream that now cut the village in two. The local army base provided frequent visits from multi-ribboned officers but no action. A mortuary had been established but that was all. It seemed the Army had been paralysed by the disaster and was unable to function. Local villagers were desperate to be reunited and so by midday our youngsters had constructed a bridge which allowed the locals and some fifty army personnel to cross.

We could now escape the village, but the locals told us that further bridges had been destroyed so there was no certainty of escape to Leh, some 20 miles away across the Himalayas. We had no idea what lay before us except that the road had disappeared and several swollen rivers would have to be navigated.

After breakfast we loaded up and moved to the first crossing which we had previously bridged. This river crossing was followed by a trek to the second crossing which again was forded with little difficulty. Beyond this was complete devastation with houses and roads completely destroyed. In places we climbed on to sections of surviving road which were now perched over 20ft above the ground.

After some hours the first mountain pass was spotted and at the summit the Indian Army dispensed tea and curry to weary survivors. The group then trekked on down into the Leh Valley and another river crossing, undertaken at speed amongst a crowd desperate to escape. A road was quickly reached and a truck took us to the destroyed

Young adventurers survey the damage

army base at Pang where a huge steel Bailey bridge had been tossed 200m downstream by the deluge. In its place three steel ladders had been strung together to span the major river. Balancing on the ladders and clutching a rope, the group finally gained access to the road to Leh.

The aftermath

The devastation brought by the storm upon the Ladakh region was considerable. Occurring in one of the driest inhabited areas on earth it was unprecedented. In a very sparsely populated area over 1000 people died. The very nature of the destruction, wiping out whole neighbourhoods and villages, meant there was often no one left to inform the authorities. We do know whole road-repair gangs disappeared and eight days after the deluge the army discovered they had lost a border post with twenty six men in it. Inevitably the real casualties were the Ladakhis. In Leh whole areas of the town were devastated. The bus station, power station and the hospital were all

Crossing a makeshift ladder bridge to reach Leh

destroyed. All roads were washed away, bridges were gone and a Tibetan orphanage was destroyed.

After some four days, and an extended wait at the airport amongst hundreds of desperate people trying to escape the town, we finally managed to board an emergency Air India flight to Delhi.

Note: Leh, the capital of Ladakh, has the highest airfield in the world. This is the coldest and highest inhabited place on earth, isolated for eight months of the year by the high peaks and populated by Buddhist nomadic herdsmen.

The Dorset Expeditionary Society

THE adventure recounted was a 'Moonlands' expedition, organised by The Dorset Expeditionary Society as one of many opportunities offered to young people in far flung areas of the world, including Bolivia, Canada, China, Ecuador, Iceland, India, Peru and Thailand.

A registered charity, the DES was established in our County some thirty years ago and during that time has supported the development of many thousands of youngsters, including those disadvantaged and disaffected, in adventurous activities - by challenging them to seek personal qualities of service, leadership and self-sufficiency. Sponsorship is provided to help the financially disadvantaged and programmes are set so young people work together, respect each other and accept responsibility for their actions.

Since 1985, in addition to thousands of UK ventures, the DES has fielded some 100 expeditions to 24 countries across four continents.

Editor's note: The writer, John Hegarty, a member of the Society of Dorset Men, has led nearly 60 of the expeditions. His previous ventures have received both the Karrimor and Sir Vivian Fuchs Awards. He is a Churchill Fellow, a Fellow of both the Royal Society of Arts and the Royal Geographical Society, has served as a member of the National Council of Young Explorers Trust, is a College Vice Principal, holds a commission in the Territorial Army and is a Duke of Edinburgh's Award Gold Expedition Assessor. John is also a Plato Award holder and helped to establish the Dorset Expeditionary Society.

Which one is the ALIEN?

The picture on the left of course!
but that on the right is a little alien too.

What is a 15th century effigy of a 'cadaver on a table tomb' doing in a predominantly 19th century church - St. Mary's at Stalbridge?

Answers on a postcard please. . .

(picture credits: The Editor & Google Images)

The Rifles

Keeping up-to-date with the Regiment by Lieutenant Colonel Geoff Nicholls

The Rifles Regimental Badge

WITH enormous pleasure I can state that, when writing, the past year has been the first in the relatively short life of the Regiment during which we have suffered no fatalities through enemy action. This has come as a great relief and is a sign of the diminishing importance with which Afghanistan is being viewed by HM Government as the troops gradually pull out. Nonetheless, we still have two battalions heavily involved in the campaign and it is very likely that 5 Rifles, who were the last unit in Iraq, may well be the last in Afghanistan. Whether this is a matter for pride and celebration, or simply a coincidence, is open to discussion.

The Rifles – Locally

In Dorset there have been a number of memorable events. Unfortunately the dedication of a new War Memorial in Shaftesbury had to be postponed, but in nearby Sherborne the Regiment was officially granted the civic honour of the town in a ceremony during which the town was presented with a Silver Bugle, being the Regimental symbol.

The Sherborne bugle

The major event of the period was the exercising of the Freedom of Bridport. Although awarded the Freedom in 2011, the Regiment had been unable to march through the centre because the battalions were all busy on operations. The earlier disappointment was quickly forgotten as the Regiment marched through the town in spectacular fashion on a suitably sunny June day.

The collection for the subsequent church service was kindly donated to the Regiment's own charity Care for Casualties; which also received generous donations from a number of other fund-raising events.

Among the former regiments of The Rifles was, of course, The Dorset Regiment and the past year has seen a number of events celebrating that great county regiment; including a Service of Remembrance held at the Tirah Memorial in Dorchester to commemorate those members of the Dorsets who took part in the campaign of 1897 in the North West Frontier District of India (now Pakistan). This was where Private Samuel Vickery won the VC for rescuing a wounded comrade

The Mayor of Bridport,
Cllr. Maggie Ray, inspects the troops

under heavy enemy fire. The Regimental Trustees recently contributed towards the renovation of the monument.

Nationally and Internationally

Let me take you through a brief summary of the activities undertaken by our seven battalions since my report in the last Year Book.

1 Rifles, having been stood down from a possible deployment to Afghanistan, then

The Tirah obelisk in Dorchester

found themselves conducting a huge variety of activities. Two companies travelled to exercise in Kenya and not long afterwards an Infantry Short-term Training Team deployed to Mali for six months as part of the EU Training Mission to assist the Mali Armed Forces. Adventurous training expeditions to Alaska, South Africa, Brunei and Corsica have been conducted. The battalion snipers took the top prizes in the Tri Service Sniper Competition on Salisbury Plain, maintaining the understandable historical importance of shooting in a regiment called "The Rifles".

LCpl Matthew Wilson from **2 Rifles** was presented with the Military Special Recognition Award at the Pride of Britain ceremony in London. While deployed in

Afghanistan he ran across open ground in full view of the enemy to assist a wounded comrade. As he ran, a sniper's bullet smashed into his helmet, knocking him out for 30 seconds. When he came to, he saw that a helicopter, trying to rescue casualties, was under fire. He ran 50 metres across open ground to attack the enemy and draw fire away from the helicopter. His award was presented to him by singer Katherine Jenkins and comedian Michael McIntyre.

While some of **3 Rifles** went off to sunnier climes in Kenya, where they were briefly marooned due to internal political issues, a company deployed in a rather colder direction; south to the Falklands for their new role as the Resident Infantry Company. Highlights for them included painting The Bugle on a hillside near the camp which can be seen on Google Earth!

4 Rifles deployed to Afghanistan for six months under command of Brigadier Rupert Jones, an Old Shirburnian. He is now Commander 1 Infantry Brigade.

5 Rifles conducted considerable military training in Bavaria where they experienced record rainfall and floods and have subsequently deployed to a very dry Afghanistan.

Infantry training in Mali

6 Rifles had been ready to mobilise up to 50 Riflemen to deploy to Afghanistan alongside 1 Rifles but this was cancelled and they were fortunate to be able to take advantage of many 'betterment' measures now on offer to the Reserves, including a summer deployment to Cyprus, culminating in a beach landing and inevitable dawn attack.

The highlight of **7 Rifles** year was an exercise with the Danish Home Guard in Jutland.

Back to Dorset

Many readers will be aware that the ambulatory in Sherborne Abbey is, in effect, the Dorset Regiment's Chapel. The Abbey authorities have agreed to allow a number of artefacts from the Devonshire and Dorset Regiment – two pairs of Colours, a Regimental badge and a new cabinet to house the various Books of Remembrance - to be placed in the Chapel.

A new history of the Dorsets, covering the Second World War and post-war years, entitled "They couldn't have done better", will , on publication, be available in' good book shops' and the Keep Military Museum in Dorchester. It promises to be an excellent read.

THE HANGMAN INN

Young farmers back from college tasks; swilling ale from polished casks
The wounded soldier home from war showing everyone his scar
The guarded Masons' room above; Charity and brotherly love
The drooling Squire, red in face, the barmaid's bodice, undone lace
At tavern door the hunters meet impatient hounds, the fox to beat
Parsnip Polly on the floor; the barmaid serving her no more
The mysterious lady, French escort; disembarked at Weymouth Port

The landlord gross, with florid face dancing on the table
Made dancers of the human race as the hangman, Martin Stable
He loved to watch the dance of death; legs kicking in the air
The tongue protruding from the head, the eyes with bloodshot stare
His grisly business he enjoyed, with halter, blindfold, tiers
The courts to keep him full employed was all that he desired
To measure men was his delight and good at calculation
He'd check their health, their weight, their height
Prepare them for damnation
Highwaymen, robbers of the mail were hung by Martin proud
His trusty halter never failed to entertain the crowd
Retirement as a hangman bold he took this old coach – house
He changed the name in letters gold
From the renowned "Roach and Grouse"

Albert Douglas Gillen

THE POWYS SOCIETY

The 2014 annual report by Hon. Secretary Chris Thomas

THE Powys Society annual conference, which this year was called "To Chart the Powys World", was held on 15th to 17th August at the Sherborne Hotel in Sherborne. Over 50 members registered for a packed programme of talks and organised walks. There were plenty of opportunities to explore places associated with the Powys family such as the Abbey, the almshouses, the Castle, the "Slopes", the Trent Lanes and Sherborne School as well as visit other Powysian places such as Bradford Abbas and Weymouth.

The Sherborne connection

Sherborne was very well known to the Powyses and references to the town, the surrounding countryside and its field paths, frequently appear in their books. In his memoirs, The Joy of It (1937) and Still the Joy of It (1956), Littleton Powys recounted his very happy life as a schoolboy and later as a schoolmaster and headmaster of Sherborne Prep. as well as his life with his first wife, Mabel, when they lived in the house that his brother ARP, built for them in Sherborne which they called Quarry House.

The Dorset and Somerset Essays by Llewelyn are full of notes on Sherborne. In an evocative essay, The River Yeo, Llewelyn wrote: "...Sherborne in the early summer is without doubt 'the flour of Cities all' in Dorset" and quoted from John Leland's Itinerary "I take it to be the best towne at this present tyme in Dorsetshire."

John Cowper Powys felt a special connection with the town. He vividly described his schooldays there in Autobiography, and, of course, memorably depicted the town as Ramsgard in his novel Wolf Solent (1929), including a wonderful description of the fan tracery of the Abbey roof, redolent with suggestive imagery, that could only have been produced by someone with a long and intimate acquaintance with the building: "Wolf contemplated once more that famous fan tracery roof. Those lovely organic lines and curves, up there in the greenish dimness challenged something in his soul... This high fan tracery roof, into whose creation so much calm mysticism must have been thrown seemed to appeal with an almost personal sympathy to Wolf's deepest mind." He goes on to describe the effect of the fan tracery on Wolf's soul: "Uplifted there, in the immense stillness of that enclosed space, it seemed to fling forth, like some great ancient fountain in a walled garden, eternal arches of enchanted water that sustained, comforted and healed."

But perhaps, most powerful of all, John Cowper Powys gave a very personal account of his relationship to Sherborne, whilst living in the USA, as a writer in exile, in the introduction to the edition of Wolf Solent published in 1961: "As I wrote Wolf Solent travelling through all the states of the United Sates, except two, I became more and more intensely aware of the hills and valleys, the trees and various flowers, the lanes and hedges, and ponds and ditches, of the country round Sherborne; with the Abbey and the Preparatory School and the Big School; and also of the Great House and Lake, a mile or so away."

It was easy to feel, at the conference, that we had returned to the actual source of creative inspiration for the Powyses, their fons et origo, a place where images of topography, townscapes, landscape, and the memories of childhood merged and flowed freely into their writing: "Dorsetshire seems to have got hold of me" says Wolf Solent in an echo of the author's own feelings. Wolf identifies with the landscape and becomes all the things that he sees:"I am Melbury Bub. I am Blackmore Vale and High Stoy"

John Cowper Powys and Llewelyn never forgot that the inspiration they consistently drew from included a particular indebtedness to Thomas Hardy whose presence they felt with great intensity. John Cowper Powys dedicated his first novel Wood and Stone (1915) to Hardy "the monarch of that particular country" (Wessex) whilst Llewelyn wrote a deeply felt dedication to Hardy in Thirteen Worthies (1923):"whose footfalls...

The brothers circa 1901 – John Cowper, Littleton, Theodore, Albert, Llewelyn and William.

indent the turnpike roads, the honeysuckle lanes, the flinty ewe cropped downs of the ancient county of Dorset in England."

Hyman on G. Wilson Knight

The conference commenced with a vibrant talk delivered by our Chairman, Timothy Hyman, artist, RA, and author, about his acquaintance with the writer, friend of John Cowper Powys, founding member and President of the Powys Society and famous Shakespearian scholar, producer and actor, G. Wilson Knight (1897-1985). Timothy first met Wilson Knight when he was still an art student at the Slade, aged 26, and Wilson Knight was an elderly statesman like man of 75. Timothy entertained us with a fund of stories and anecdotes about Wilson Knight's idiosyncratic way of life and his strongly held personal beliefs as well as giving us an insight into his ideas about the leading Saturnian theme in John Cowper Powys's books. Wilson Knight's book, The Saturnian Quest (1964), is still one of the best introductions both to the work of John Cowper Powys as well as to Wilson Knight's method of "interpretation" which he originally developed at the beginning of his academic career in a book about Shakespeare's tragedies, The Wheel of Fire (1930), which includes an introduction and endorsement by T.S. Eliot. Wilson Knight was a prolific writer and produced books on religion and philosophy as well as many books and essays on literary interpretation. In every book he wrote he never failed to find space to champion the work of his friend John Cowper Powys, with whom he shared a special affinity. In his strange, late, book, Symbol of Man: on Body-Soul for stage and studio (1979), he posed naked for photographic illustrations to demonstrate the meaning of certain grand dramatic gestures. Here he stated quite categorically: "My admiration for Powys is boundless."

Our Vice-Chairman, Peter Foss, author of A Bibliography of Llewelyn Powys (2007) and many other books and articles about the Powyses, presented a highly informative talk about Llewelyn Powys, illustrated with numerous images of Davos in Switzerland where Llewelyn stayed at a sanatorium for treatment of TB and where he was visited by members of his family and other famous people such as the artist Ludwig Kirchner and the writer and translator, Arthur Waley. Marcella Henderson-Peal, lecturer in English at the University of Paris, talked about her researches into the reception in France by French writers, philosophers and intellectuals in the 1930s, such as Jean Wahl, Gaston Bachelard as well as Jean Paul Sartre and Simone de Beauvoir. Jonathan Goodwin, Assistant Professor of English at the University of Louisiana at Lafayette, came all the way from the USA to present a talk on John Cowper Powys's late novel Atlantis (1954), a work which is rarely discussed but is full of Homeric magic and Greek mythological figures which Powys adored so much.

Sherborne towards Yeovil

On Saturday afternoon, the second day of the conference, some members followed the field path from Sherborne toward Yeovil, which runs adjacent to the Bradford Abbas road, and the river Yeo, a route which was frequently travelled by John Cowper Powys using the railway which passes nearby. This part of Dorset is described with unfailing enthusiasm and rapture by Powys in the early part of Wolf Solent: "What a country this was! To his right...the ground sloped upwards, cornfield after cornfield of young green shoots...To his left the Vale of Blackmore beckoned to him out of its meadows.." We had come this way to visit Wyke Manor, situated about half way between Sherborne and Yeovil, especially to investigate whether this might be one of the original inspirations for the description of Kings Barton Manor in Wolf Solent. However it was hard to reconcile the smallish manor we found with John Cowper Powys's description, in the introduction to the novel, of a "castellated House" and a "big house" with a "large library". But the location of the house close to Bradford Abbas (Kings Barton in Wolf Solent) and Powys's description elsewhere in the novel of "a small and unimportant building" and a description of the drive entrance to the house: "it was not a long drive and it did not lead to a big house" all seemed to make a perfect fit. Powys's reference to mullioned windows, heraldic images, and a big library as well as other internal and external features could easily have been combined with features derived from other large country houses in the area such as Newton Surmaville,near Yeovil, Clifton Maybank as well as Montacute House. It is likely that even the sinister Squire Urquhart, in Wolf Solent, may have been inspired by a local antiquarian and historian, E.H.Bates Harbin (1862-1918), who was President of the Somerset Archaeology and Natural History Society, lived at Newton Surmaville and owned a large library of books. Wyke Manor is a house of considerable historic interest

The Powys Brothers : John Cowper – Theodore Francis – Llewelyn

and is just the kind of ancient building likely to have appealed to John Cowper Powys. The house was built in 1650, preserves many of its original stonework, doors and porticoes and is mentioned in Pevsner's survey of the buildings of Dorset. Our hosts, the present tenants, were very gracious, kind and generous. They told us about the connection of the house with Winchester College and served us tea in their beautiful garden surrounded by the remains of a moat and trailing, wild plants, flowers and open, flat, fields.

Back to School

Back at the conference venue we were given a rare opportunity to inspect copies of original material from the archives of Sherborne School, compiled by the school archivist, who had very kindly produced photocopies of some of the pupil records of the Powyses, as well as admission registers, letters, newspaper cuttings, photographs, the titles of books borrowed by the Powyses, off-prints of the school magazine, The Shirburnian and an extract from John Cowper Powys's winning English essay prize in 1891 entitled: Ancient Compared with Modern Ideals of Patriotism, showing an early use of Powys's predilection for the exclamation mark.

Moonfleet, Chesil Beach and Chaldon

On Saturday 19 July the Powys Society hosted a meeting in the library of the Dorset Natural History and Archaeological Society, at the Dorset County Museum in Dorchester. We were delighted to welcome Kenneth Hillier, founder and Secretary of the John Meade Falkner Society who talked to us about the life and career of Falkner (1858-1932), poet, novelist, businessman and author of topographical guides and scholarly works on palaeography, whose father was curate of Holy Trinity church in Dorchester, and later of Buckland Ripers near Weymouth. As a boy John Meade Falkner lived in Dorchester and Weymouth, knew many of the places loved by the Powyses and wrote three novels all of which have settings in rural Dorset – The Lost Stradivarius (1895), Moonfleet (1898) and The Nebuly Coat (1903) - a novel which bears a strong resemblance to William Golding's modern novel The Spire. In the afternoon Kenneth took us on a guided tour of the old church at Fleet, near Abbotsbury, close to where John Cowper Powys's ashes were scattered on Chesil beach. Fleet old church provided Falkner with the setting for his most famous novel, about smuggling, Moonfleet. The original church, however, was devastated and overwhelmed by the encroaching sea in the terrible storm of 1824 and now only survives as a tiny chapel. It is beautifully situated amidst tall trees, green fields, and within sight of the sea and Chesil bank.

Last year marked the 130th birthday of Llewelyn Powys. Our partners, the Dandelion Fellowhship, dedicated to celebrating the work of Llewelyn Powys, organised the 19th year of the Llewelyn birthday walk on August 13th.. Members gathered at the Sailors

Return in East Chaldon to honour Llewelyn and, led by Neil Atkin Lee, the founder of the Dandelion Fellowship, walked, in very stormy weather, to Chydyok on the downs, a place full of Powysian memories and the ghosts of the past, and then to Llewelyn's memorial stone and the coastguard cottages.

In May the Powys Society travelled to Paris where we very successfully launched, at the famous bookshop, Shakespeare and Co, on the left bank, a new book, published by the Powys Press, called Proteus and the Magician – the letters of Henry Miller and John Cowper Powys. The launch coincided with a festival, organised by the Henry Miller Memorial Library in Big Sur in California, aimed at celebrating Miller's association with Paris. The book has been edited by our colleague in France, Jacqueline Peltier, editor of la letter powysienne, and includes an introduction, extensive explanatory notes, a bibliography and index. This is the first time the complete correspondence between Powys and Miller has been published in one place in English.

County Museum & Exeter University

Our year was dominated by negotiations to transfer the Powys Society Collection from the Dorset County Museum in Dorchester to the University of Exeter. This has now been completed. Researchers and members of the public may inspect items from the Collection freely on application to the Special Archives Collections at Exeter. We will of course continue to maintain our connections with the Dorset County Museum where we still have a presence in the Writer's Gallery. We have also donated many objects to the Museum associated with the Powys family including the paintings and sketches of Gertrude Powys. The Director of the Dorset County Museum, Jon Murden, says that he hopes to organise an exhibition of Gertrude's work at the Museum in the near future.

We are making plans for this year and expect to hold meetings in Montacute, Dorchester, and London. All our meetings are free and everyone is welcome to attend. We are always delighted to welcome new members. Our annual 2015 conference will take place in Llangollen, in Wales, between 21 to 23 August.

If you would like to find out more about our activities or join the Powys Society please visit our web site: www.powys-society.org, contact the Hon. Secretary by e-mail at chris.d.thomas@hotmail.co.uk or write to Chris Thomas, Hon. Secretary, The Powys Society, Flat D, 87 Ledbury Road, London W11 2AG.

The Powys Society is a registered charity(801332). The Society as founded in 1967 with the aim of promoting public education and recognition of the writings, thought and contribution to the arts, of the Powys family, particularly of John Cowper Powys, Theodore and Llewelyn Powys. The Society is international, attracts scholars and general readers from around the world and welcomes anyone interested in learning more about this very talented and unusual family.

Ivy Gale – a lifetime of memories in Dorchester

Surviving hard times in the "wrong end of town" as told to David Forrester

IVY was born in 1917, when war was raging across Europe but all was quiet in Fordington. She lived in the centre cottage of a terrace of three cottages, 10 Standfast Road, which no longer exists

Ivy told me, "Our cottages were one room up and one room down. Single ladies lived either side of us but our cottage was somewhat more crowded. I was the middle one of seven sisters, two of whom died. We all lived in the one room downstairs, then at night we all slept in the one room upstairs, us girls all in one bed, three across the top of the bed, two across the bottom. We continued these sleeping arrangements until two of the girls reached puberty, at which time the girls were moved out, one to stay with Granny and the other to stay with Dad's sister.

The cottages we lived in were served by one outside tap and one outside toilet between the three cottages."

"My mother, Jane, managed all the cooking, heating pots over an open fire in the downstairs room. Once a week a long bath was brought in from the yard, kettles and pots were boiled and the whole family bathed in turn."

The last surviving of the children Ivy remembers her cottage faced the back of St. George's graveyard. "Here a great number of my family were buried," said Ivy. "They are all up one side of the path. The caretaker at the cemetery at that time was Mr. Walton."

Ivy's grandmother was a Voss and lived in Holloway Road while her other grandparents, the Gales, lived in Cokers Frome. They were later to become a very important lifeline for Ivy.

All roads lead to home

"My father John was a steam roller driver for Eddisons, a big company based

A 1920s shepherd's hut

in Wareham Road, Fordington, so he worked away a lot. He would tow a shepherd's-type hut behind his machine in which to spend the night. Every few weeks I would travel, with my mum, to take Dad clean clothes. I was a Daddy's girl really."

Eddisons had contracts to mend and build roads all over Dorset. John's machine had a device fitted to the side which would tear up the surface of old roads. This would be cleared away and the new surface laid down and rolled in.

"Unfortunately, when I was quite young, my father had a bad accident," said Ivy. "He was in hospital for a year and, at this time, also developed a weak heart."

This put an enormous burden on Ivy's mother as John never really worked again. There was no social security so you were on your own. Jane took in washing and worked at the Union to make ends meet, though Ivy never went hungry. "We never ate just dry bread, there was always something to put on it." Ivy stressed. Jane was a good manager and hard worker but they were all fortunate to have a wider family to lean on.

"On Fridays I would go down to Eddisons with my little trolley to meet the carrier who would bring a sack of vegetables from Granny and Grandad Gale. The vegetables would get us through the week but a sixpenny piece, always sewn into the top corner of the bag, was a huge help in those days.

"Once a week my sister and I would visit the Moule Institute where the ladies of the church would give us two long loaves of bread. We couldn't have managed without the ladies of the church."

It is interesting that John, as a Salvationist, was very strict, never smoked or drank. Jane was Welsh and a Methodist and refused to change to the Salvation Army. It is clear that none of this stood in the way of the help being given by the Church at the Moule Institute (now sadly demolished).

Singing and messing about in the river

From a very early age Ivy discovered that, like her mother, she had a voice. "At the age of five I was sitting on the stage at the Corn Exchange with a basket of flowers singing Will you buy my pretty flowers? I have always had a voice and sang in choirs but now my voice is gone and I can't sing anymore."

Despite living in abject poverty, Ivy's mother was determined that they should all have clean clothes and a starched pinafore. When Ivy was four, she and her sisters were fishing with a jam jar by the mill when she was pushed over by a bigger boy and floated off down the river, supported by the air trapped under her starched pinny. The current was quite fast and Ivy was carried along until spotted by a sharp-eyed woman from the 'Big House' on the corner, who pulled her out before she was swept off through the hatches. Ivy, of course, cannot remember this but the story was related to her by her parents.

School

Ivy told me, "I attended St. George's Infants School at the top of High Street from the age of three. Sometimes I had a problem as I couldn't pull my knickers up properly or tie up my boots.

Occasionally I would have to run off down Holloway Road, knickers around my ankles and boots in hand, for Granny Voss to sort me out."

"When aged seven I moved on to the Gasworks School in Icen Way," said Ivy. "When we needed coke I would take my little trolley to school so that I could take a sack of coke back home."

Dorchester Gasworks School

"Times being so hard, nothing would be expected at Christmas," Ivy explained. "However, we never went without. We each had a black stocking with an orange, apples or perhaps a pear and some fruit cake. There was always a silver threepenny piece sewn into the top." Supplied by the grandparents, this has become a tradition for the family, continued first by Ivy and now by her daughter.

Max Gate - as it is now

During Ivy's school days many children suffered from diphtheria. " A number of the parents thought it came from using the swimming baths at Grey's Bridge which were then closed." Ivy explained. These were fed with river water, a health hazard caused by cows in the river upstream.

Ivy went down with diphtheria and was, with many others, put into the isolation hospital in Herringstone Road, a series of old timber buildings with tin roofs. Ivy remembers it well. "It was totally overcrowded, the beds were side by side with hardly any room to move. I think I was about ten at the time."

Was Hardy 'orrible ?

By the age of eight Ivy had moved to Fordington Hill and was busy doing lots of jobs for her mother.

"Twice a week I would take my little cart loaded with clean washing to Max Gate for the Hardys. My two sisters, Nelly and Bessie, were at this time working for Thomas Hardy, one as a chambermaid, the other in the kitchen. Thomas Hardy would often see me as I walked through the garden with my little cart, but never once spoke or gave me a smile. Mrs. Hardy though always made a fuss of me and would give me a piece of fruit."

Life was hard for the two girls in service and days were long. "Mr. Hardy was prone to follow the chambermaids around and would often remove coal from a newly made-up fire," Ivy explained. "When it came to meal times, he controlled how much the staff could eat. The cook was not allowed to have the remains of a joint. He would carve a slice each for the staff and then it was put away!"

Then came that fateful day – 11th January 1928.

Ivy told me, "I was now aged eleven and arrived as usual with the washing. My sister ran to meet me. 'You can't come round to the kitchen,' she said. 'Come around the side. The old man has died and they're all in the kitchen with him."

"Well," Ivy continued, "as it turned out, Thomas Hardy's heart was removed there and then and put into an OXO tin, from there it was transferred into a casket supplied by the undertaker and taken to Stinsford Vicarage until it was put into the grave."

"Once the OXO tin was empty, Mrs Hardy made the gardener dig a deep hole in a far corner of the garden and bury it. I could still point out where the tin was buried."

Presumably this was to stop anyone taking it as a memento. A popular story at the time was a fallacy because Ivy continued, "The cat never did eat his heart."

She added about Thomas Hardy "There's not much good to be said about him." I am not surprised as his last housekeeper once said to me "Horrible man!"

In deep water for being late home

As a teenager Ivy remembered, "With my sister, I used to go to dances. There were two rules. We had to be back home by nine O'clock and we must not dance with soldiers. The second rule we often broke as we loved dancing with soldiers but they wore white belts and the white came off onto our dresses while dancing close! So a routine developed. We would stand outside a nearby shop and rub the white off our dresses and inspect each other before entering the house."

John had a soft spot for the girls and would often overlook lateness. "As our house was built up against a builder's yard it made it possible to get over the low wall, on to the lid of the water butt and in through our bedroom window," said Ivy. And so they often avoided discovery. Ivy said her mother would say " 'Those girls are late again John,' but Good old Dad, having heard us creep in, would reply 'Oh no Jane, they're upstairs in bed' ".

After a while, however, John decided this had to stop. Unknown to the girls, he removed the lid from the water butt. Ivy remembered, grinning, "We arrived home and made our usual entrance. I stepped over the wall and straight into deep water! I had no choice but to wring out my clothes as best I could and hide them under other clothes ready for the wash."

The next morning their father said, "Lot of noise out the back last night!" Ivy replied, quick as a flash. "That must have been old Tom the cat again." But the game was up.

William and Ivy on their wedding day

70 years of marriage

Ivy married a 20 year-old soldier, William Hain from Yeovil, when she was eighteen but her hard life was not over.

"My husband was in Bomb Disposal and was damaged in the neck by shrapnel. At the time I was a sergeant driving a lorry which carried a barrage balloon. I had my 21st birthday about this time but didn't really know it until a card arrived from my mother. "

"Despite my husband's injuries, he was a bus driver for many years until he was unable to work due to his health. He eventually went blind and I had to nurse him. He lived until he was 90 but I continued to nurse him at home for many years. Finally he went into hospital for the last year of his life as I was not allowed to have him at home. This made me very sad as they didn't think I could continue looking after him , even though I wanted to."

William and Ivy during the war

During the interview Ivy made it clear that "despite living just around the corner we were not allowed down into Mill Street as it was considered far too rough for young girls."

Interestingly, I am now working with the Mill Street Housing Society, recording the memories of people who lived, or knew relatives, in Mill Street – when it was 'the wrong end of town'. Eventually, I hope to produce a book, to be published by Roving Press, based on these memories. If you can help please contact me on 01305 250882.

Editor's note: David is the author of the much acclaimed FORDINGTON REMEMBERED: Growing up in and around Dorchester. Published by Roving Press at only £6.99, ISBN 978-1-906651-237

Keep on the right side. . . or should that be left?

Have a little chuckle – care of Hayne Russell

Two locals were enjoying their pint in the village pub.

"Where be goin' ver these 'oliday then Wilf ?" asked George.

"Well," said Wilf, "Fer the fust time I an' Missus thought us'd go to France."

"Be goin' be bus?" asked George.   "No, I be thinken o' drivin" replied Wilf.

"Ah well, these knowed they drive tother zide over there don 'ee" said George.

"Ah right!" said Wilf.

Some time later they met again in the pub.

George said " 'Ow did 'ee git on over in France then Wilf ?"

"Did'n go!" said Wilf.   "Wass 'appened then?" asked George.

"Well, atter what you zed to I las' time, I took Missus wi' I ver a practise drive up on thick Motorway. Us decided tis too b..... dangerous!"

Bizarre ballooning over Bridport

*Richard J Fox MBE tells the story of an 1881 disaster
and his own ballooning venture in Lyme Bay*

TOWARDS the end of the 19th century British Military establishments were experimenting with hot air balloons. The Navy was especially interested in the composition of clouds and the changes of barometric pressure within them. It was decided by the Admiralty to utilise a hot air balloon, suitably equipped with appropriate measuring devices, to be released from the Naval land base in Bath, for a weather research flight for the Meteorological Society.

Their Lordships put their proposal to the House of Commons. This was agreed but with the proviso that an official observer should be in attendance. The MP for Malmesbury, Walter Powell, volunteered and was unanimously accepted.

Walter Powell
and Capt. James Templer

Walter Powell was already a celebrated aeronaut and on 10th December 1881 he joined Captain James Templer, a pioneer in military ballooning, and his assistant A. Agg-Gardner, in the basket of SALADIN; a balloon filled with 38,000 feet of 'used coal gas', rather than expensive hydrogen, and measuring 60 feet long by 30 feet wide.

The three intrepid adventurers rose to a considerable height and disappeared into the clouds.

Without warning the wind changed direction. The balloon picked up speed and drifted across Glastonbury, Crewkerne and over Beaminster. Cloud prevented visual course correction and they were overhead of Bridport before taking urgent measures to reduce height.

An emergency touchdown was attempted in a field directly behind the cliff overlooking West Bay. The landing was uncontrolled and violent. James Templer was thrown out of the basket on impact and Agg-Gardner was caught in a rope and dragged along the ground, breaking his leg.

With such a loss of weight the balloon rose quickly into the air with the MP stalwartly remaining in the basket and the other two intrepid seafarers watching helplessly as he disappeared over the horizon towards France.

THE ACCIDENT TO THE "SALADIN" NEAR BRIDPORT, DORSETSHIRE, AS SEEN BY THE ONLY EYE-WITNESS

From The Graphic - 17th December 1881

Messages were dispatched, a general search was made but no trace of the balloon could be established. A week later a message was received from Spain that wreckage, thought to be Saladin, was found on the slopes of the Pyrenees. The body of the MP was never found.

Life Boat week in Lyme Regis

Years ago I was a member of the Lyme Regis life boat crew. Each year the last week in July is Life Boat week and many events are held to raise money for the RNLI. In the mid 1970s I was the event's organiser.

By chance I came across an article on 'how to make small tissue paper balloons' in an old National Geographical magazine and my first experiment worked quite well. I became more ambitious and made a bigger one which was misshapen and flew rather precariously. Finally I got the design right with the glue joining the segments together creating a strong frame for the flimsy tissue paper.

It was decided to fly one of my balloons on each of the days of Life Boat Week with sponsors having the opportunity to advertise their company logo on their balloon.

Among those who took up the offer were Renault Cars, Babycham and Westland Aircraft.

It took several months to complete the construction programme with each balloon being over 20 ft. high. As so Life Boat Week commenced.

Inflated and full of hot air

Westland Aircraft sent a support team, complete with a caravan, and stayed all week.

Each afternoon hundreds of holiday makers and locals enjoyed the spectacle of a large unmanned balloon taking off and floating gently out to sea and over the horizon.

Westland's turn came on the Friday. With great enthusiasm the team helped to inflate their large white balloon. Weather conditions seemed favourable and a gentle breeze created ripples on the paper as the monster expanded. With a great cheer it was released and slowly rose above the Marine Parade.

Suddenly and without warning a violent squall blew in from the sea. The balloon wrapped itself round a lamp-post, its hot air escaping from a large tear, and then collapsed in a heap on the tarmac. It was a complete disaster. . . . . . but fortunately no loss of life!

Richard, who has lived in Portugal for several years, served Lyme Regis as Town Crier, was greatly involved in setting up the twinning of Lyme with St. George's, Bermuda, and over many years ran various businesses in the town including the Cob Arms Hotel, Volunteer Inn, Country Stocks and a curiosity/gift shop at the top of Broad Street. He was awarded the MBE in 2006.

Richard John Fox – Town Crier
By Sydney Bodle (1979)
Photo credit: Lyme Regis Museum

Fellow Dorset Richard John Fox, a pillar of the establishment in Lyme Regis, was the Official Town Guide and conducted over 7000 people on his town walks. He retired to live in Portugal.

In 2014 Dorset Police launched a campaign to recruit more volunteer officers.
Society of Dorset Men member and local businessman Alex Smith
gives his story on being a Special Constable.

A Special Story! !

By Special Constable Alex Smith!

AS a kid I grew up with some really old technology, instead of iPads and Mobile phones we used CB-radio. My uncle Michael was a keen radio amateur and it was fascinating to watch him in his radio shack operating a big old HF transceiver and morse key. I quickly joined a local radio club and took a test to gain my own call sign. One of my favourite channels to tune in to was the local police frequency before they went digital!

When I left school in 2000 at the age of 16, I was faced with many career choices and routes. I was always intrigued by the Police Service, so decided on taking a BTEC national diploma in Public Services at the Weymouth College. When I reached 19 I decided to apply to become a regular police constable but was sadly unsuccessful at the interview due to a lack of

Following the attestation at Dorset Police HQ.

life experience. I took the feedback onboard and whilst studying at college I gained valuable experience through a number of jobs including beach control at Weymouth, static site guarding and retail security/loss prevention with Securicor!

It was around this time when I heard about the Special Constabulary at an open day at Dorset Police headquarters in Winfrith.!

I soon discovered that a Special was a fully-trained volunteer police officer with exactly the same powers and uniform. I applied for a 'patrol observer' shift where you get to go out with police officers and see exactly what they get up to - the adrenaline really started to pump when we attend a flash priority incident with the blue lights flashing and siren screaming.!

The excitement of having to deal with new situations, thinking on my feet and giving back to the local community in this extraordinary way really appealed to me. In January 2008, I applied to become a Special and following the assessment day I was offered a place on the next training course. The initial training course involved attending police headquarters each weekend for three months learning law, policing powers and how to hone my communication skills to deal with situations.! !

 That August, I was appointed, and carried out my duties as a Special Constable in Weymouth & Portland. Initially I was crewed up with an experienced regular officer or special. I can remember my first duty when we stopped a young moped rider and found several defects on his bike. The young lad wasn't too happy to receive a ticket requesting him to rectify the faults within 14-days.

Being on the frontline serving the community provides many opportunities to help people in need.

From the elderly lady who was confused and lost, to comforting two very young children that were on a protection order whilst the mother had been arrested. Most people think Specials are just used for special events such as local carnivals and cycle proficiency schemes but this is not the case in 2014! As a special you get involved in every aspect of policing including drugs warrants, neighbourhood policing, speed enforcement and attachments to specialist operations like marine and roads policing!

In February 2014, the UK experienced some really heavy storms, at short notice I was called to assist with the all night road closure at Chesil Beach, I worked alongside the Army and local council. This enabled the regular officers to continue with all the busy Friday night-time economy incidents in Weymouth town centre.

In 2012 Dorset Police undertook the largest policing operation outside London for the 2012 Olympics. I managed to commit a full week of duties mainly patrolling Olympic Village (Officers' Field) and outer zone. I have also assisted special branch with several Royal visits to Poundbury and The National Sailing Academy at Portland.

The Special Constabulary provides excellent leadership and development training to help individuals manage teams of specials and tutor newly recruited specials - all these skills are transferable, so of great benefit to my paid day job running an online print business.

As a special you'll need to work a minimum of 16-hours per month. If you really enjoy it and have a supportive family you'll probably end-up doing a duty every week and with additional training you can easily clock up over 40 hours each month.

The Police are very much changing continually with the times, with many more tools and smarter systems being introduced to help provide a better service to the public. I am looking forward to seeing more technology being introduced like mobile tablet computers that will enable officers to complete much of their paperwork on the move, and body worn CCTV cameras used to protect us by gathering key evidence for court cases.

You can follow Alex via twitter @dorsetspecial. If you would like further information on the Special Constabulary or other police volunteer opportunities, please visit the Dorset Police website at www.dorset.police.uk or contact the Volunteers Support Team on volunteersrecruitment@dorset.pnn.police.uk

Weymouth's Roller Revellers

Skating down memory lane with Patsy Trevett – now Pat Russell

FOR my 13th birthday I managed to wear down my parents into giving me a pair of roller skates. The skates were metal and fitted onto our shoes with a steel bracket – not good for the shoes. Two friends in Bath Street where I lived, Fay Webb and Beryl Bennett, also had skates and the three of us would try to master the art of skating by propelling ourselves up the street, grabbing hold of windowsills, downpipes – and anything that came to hand. Going up the street was manageable but going down the slight slope caused a lot of tumbles. We then made our way to Radipole Park Drive, where there was, and still is, a wide, flat pavement. Finally we progressed to the Esplanade which, of course was much more fun.

Living in his flat on the Esplanade was Col. C. F. "Cocker" Linnett – the Headmaster of Weymouth Grammar School. The Colonel was not amused by the antics of growing numbers of the youth of the town - most of whom he recognised - tearing up and down the Esplanade. We were warned off! A letter was written to the 'powers that be' and Weymouth Corporation agreed to hold skating sessions on the Pier Bandstand – "bring your own skates!" The Bandstand had a concrete floor and over the years there were lots of painful falls.

In the summer of 1948 – after devising a routine with much enthusiasm, and in very smart green outfits made by Beryl's Mum – Beryl, Fay and I entered the Talent Competition on the Pier Bandstand and won first prize.

Rolling skates gathered by Moss

There then followed a series of skating competitions – the idea originated by Mr Moss, the manager of the Pier Bandstand. We organised ourselves, formed a committee with Fay as secretary, and the Roller Skating Revue came into being. The first show took place 1949 with a large cast of 22, the youngest being aged six and the eldest 18. Taking part in one of the routines were seven girls – five being deemed too young to be skating in the show - Mary Baker, Anita Valente, Janice Brice, Elizabeth Rod and Madeline Pratt plus, of course, the six year old whose name I cannot remember.

We had great help from Mr Moss and also Mr Vye who encouraged and helped in many ways, as did Mr Eddie Hepworth, who followed Mr Moss as manager.

Left to right
Janice Brice, Mary Baker, Elizabeth Rod,
Sheila Plunkett,Anita Valente,
Madelaine Pratt and Fay Webb.

Thelma Smith and Pete Diment's adagio routine.

One show in 1949 attracted the largest crowd of the year – we were missing two of the boys, one being called up for National Service and the other breaking a finger in rehearsal!

Corporation help

In 1951 Bob Fox took over as manager of the Pier Bandstand and he became our most enthusiastic supporter. Through his efforts the Corporation provided the material for the costumes - made by the girls - spares for our skates - by this time we had skates with proper wooden wheels and white boots for the girls - a yearly meal at Pullingers Restaurant on the Pier followed by a visit to the Summer Show at the Alexandra Gardens. I see in one of the Echo reports that we attracted audiences of up to 3,000 – obviously a very good money-spinner for the Corporation.

We didn't think about money, none of us had very much, we just enjoyed the spills and the thrills and the applause for our efforts.

The girls routines included a 'Dutch' dance (minus the clogs), 'Soldiers of the Queen', followed by the uproarious parody of that number given by the boys, as recruits! 'Way out West' was skated to 'Can't get a man with a gun', and there were singles, duos and mixed duos. We aimed for grace and 'Tiller' styled precision. As well as making our own costumes we also chose our own music; 'Me and My Shadow', 'Waltz of Destiny', 'Petite Waltz', 'Tulips from Amsterdam', 'On the Sunny side of the Street' and of course 'The Skaters Waltz'.

Nina Wells and Patsy Trevett dance to 'Belle of the Ball'.

The boys' routines were very entertaining and sometimes a bit wild. They played hockey 'Arsenal 'arriers v Terrible Terras, baseball 'Roller Red Sox v Bandstand Bouncers' and the 'Bullfight', bull being played by Dave and Brian, the Matadors and Toreadors and the Shut-the-doors by the rest of the boys. Ken Perry did a 'jumping over obstacles' routine. He would tear around getting up to speed before jumping over some of us girls lying on the concrete! He only did this in practice – possibly once before it was vetoed – then he probably jumped over deck chairs. Pete did a very funny routine teaching a learner to skate – the learner being Ken. The boys persuaded Bob Fox to get a giant see-saw made; they skated up one side, the see-saw tipped and they came down other side at lightening speed – commonsense prevailed in those days – if you crashed you didn't do it again! Then there was Daisy the skating Cow ('Joker' Jolliffe and Pat Peaty) – after performing her 'tricks' she would make a visit in the audience and give rides to children. 'Daisy' was made by Bob, using an old pair of stage curtains from the Alexandra Gardens Theatre and a papier-

Daisy the Cow
Ken Perry, Eric Mead, Dave Robb, John Jolliffe – and inside Daisy were Brian Hardy and Dave Boram.

'Wedding on Wheels'
Left to right: Pete Diment, Pat Peaty, Thelma Smith, Patsy Trevett, John Jolliffee, Nina Wells, Pam Rugg, Sheila and Ken Perry.

mache head sculpted around a cardboard box.

There was always a grand finale – in the final years this was a 'Wedding on Wheels'. The girls put their names in a hat for the honour of being the bride. Nina won.

One year some of us girls were invited to put on a display at Bradford Peverell for the WI New Year Party for 65 children. Mr Collins of Cerne Abbas provided the music with his radiogram for the games and dancing. This was followed by our display – I remember that skating on a wooden floor was much better than concrete. We were invited because my aunt, Martha Hallett nee Trevett was a member of the Bradford Peverell WI.

We had three Comperes over the years; Peter Bowering, Bob Fox and Roger Pask.

Swing time in Weymouth

One year some of the girls skated in the Carnival Day Procession in our sailor outfits. That year the Carnival started and finished on Westway Road – so quite a skate from there, via the seafront and Weymouth & District Hospital (as it was then) back to Westway Road – just under six miles I've been told.

The visiting bands provided our music for the summer season. Looking back I think we were very lucky to enjoy the years of the 'big bands'; Harry Parry and his Orchestra, the Blue Rockets and the Harold Hudson Show Band. Bob tells me in 1951 the band was Ralph Sharon and his Orchestra; later Ralph Sharon became musical director to Tony Bennett – responsible for the arrangement of Tony's No 1 hit 'I left my Heart in San Francisco'. There was a season of Military Bands – a different regiment band fortnightly for twelve weeks. Apart from the military these bands had a minimum of three singers or soloists, and their leaders had no trouble providing music for our shows; the vocalist with the Royal Corps of Signals was a very young Vince Hill.

The last Revue took place in 1956 – quite a few of the original skaters had moved on with their lives – I got on a ship at Liverpool and went to Canada for the couple of years.

Having been back in Weymouth for many years I am still in contact with some of the skaters and would like to thank them for their help – and their memories – so 'thank you' to Nina, Thelma, Fay, Mary, Roger and Pete and a very big 'thank you' to

Weymouth Carnival 1952
Left to right: Patsy Trevett, Josie Basso,
Thelma Smith, Rita Roffe, Nina Wells,
June Hanger, Pam Rugg and Annette Day

Bob Fox for providing many otherwise forgotten nuggets of 'blasts from the past' and checking the piece for accuracy.

Those taking part in no particular order or year – Fay Webb, Nina Wells, Sheila Plunkett, Thelma Smith, Mary Baker, Josie Basso, Anita Valente, Janice Brice, Madeleine Pratt, Elizabeth Rod, Rita Roffe, Pam Rugg, Rosemary Ryan, June Hangar, Annette Day, Pete Diment, Ken Perry, Roger Hellaby, Peter 'Tiger' Anthony, Eric 'Ticker' Mead, Dave Boram, Ray 'Dab' Chalker, Richard Clarke, Harry Clarke, John Clarke, Dave Robb, Brian Hardy, John 'Joker' Jolliffe, Pat 'Crow' Peaty, John Tinsley, Keith Davis and yours truly Patsy Trevett.

All memories are different but mine are of lots of fun, friendships that are still ongoing and working as a team. There were no 'stars' as such but maybe 'Daisy the Comedy Cow' fitted the bill, as she doubled as the bull in the Bull Fight!

A Lyme Regis walk through history

Recommended by Julie Musk of Roving Press and abridged by her from the book of walks "Lesser Known Lyme Regis" by Joanna Smith

The Mill Walk

This walk takes you past five watermills that stood on the banks of the River Lym.

Start: Town Mill

Finish: Old Black Dog Guesthouse, Uplyme

Terrain: Slopes gently upwards beside river along paved footpath; some off-road and steep fields

Approx. distance: 2.2 km (with shorter 1.7 km return to Town Mill)

History of Town Mill

THERE is likely to have been a mill on this site since before the Domesday Book, but the first solid evidence relating to one dates from 1340 when King Edward III granted the town a licence to build a new mill. Town Mill has been owned by the borough for most of its history – hence its name.

When Lyme was besieged by Royalists in 1644, they left 'scarce a house in the whole town that was not battered'. Afterwards the government gave money to restore the town, and the stone walls of the mill that we see today were built in 1648. The four-storey miller's house was added in 1661. Major changes were made at the end of the 18th century when a bigger wheel was installed inside and a massive oak upright shaft with timber gear mounted on top, thought to date back to this time. In 1838, the mill was sold into private hands for the first time, and seems to have thrived.

Towards the end of the 19th century, small watermills faced stiff competition from engine-powered roller mills in large ports such as Plymouth and Southampton. Town Mill was finally forced out of business in 1926, and no buyer was found. The town council bought the mill back in 1929 and the buildings began an inglorious period as a depot, housing the council's traction engine and dust cart. The mill began to decay and became a popular playground for local children. Dick Hitchcock, born in 1925, remembers prising cogs from the crown wheel. 'They were apple wood and soaked in grease,' he said. 'Used to burn lovely.'

At the end of the 1950s, the Lyme Regis Silver Band practised in a tiny upstairs room off the courtyard. Band members recall sitting packed together, enveloped in thick smoke that billowed out of an inefficient pot-bellied stove. The room was freezing cold with the river visible beneath gaps in the floorboards. When a structural survey was carried out in the 1990s, 12 sticks of dynamite were discovered beneath these boards. Dynamite had been stored at the mill when the cement factory was blown up in 1936. Band members shudder when they recall how they used to drop their cigarette butts through gaps in the floorboards.

By the 1970s the mill was derelict. When it was pointed out to West Dorset District Council that they were duty bound to maintain this listed building, their response was to throw a huge tarpaulin over the entire structure. When they announced their plans to demolish the mill and sell the site for redevelopment, a small group of locals got together to save the buildings.

In 1991, the Town Mill Trust was set up to renovate the buildings for the benefit of the people of Lyme and return the mill to working order. The council handed the mill over, realising it would be more expensive to demolish the mill than maintain it. The Trust was very capably led by David West and fortunate to have the support of John Fowles and distinguished geologist Muriel Arber. A 10-year project costing £800,000 restored the Mill to the thriving centre you see today. In 2001, John Fowles opened it to the public and the first bag of flour for 75 years was ground.

Today you can see millers at work, potters at their wheels, garments being designed at the Sewing Sanctuary and hats made at the Milliner's Studio and Shop. You can visit Lyme's award-winning Cheesemonger, watch the brewer at work at the Micro-Brewery, have a glass of real ale in the courtyard, a meal at the Café and Supper Club, or simply sit and relax in the peaceful Miller's Garden. There is also a constantly changing programme of exhibitions in two beautiful galleries run by the Town Mill Arts Guild.

Behind the bustling courtyard is the 18th-century Miller's Garden. Enclosed by ancient stone walls, the garden is overflowing with herbs, fruit, flowers, vegetables

Town Mill

and medicinal plants, most of which would have been available in the 17th century. The garden is maintained by a small team of enthusiasts – new members are always welcome.

The Malthouse stands across the river from the miller's house. In 1909, the building was converted into the town's electricity generating station, housing four generators powered by noisy diesel engines; these were finally silenced in 1947 when a fire destroyed the Malthouse roof and most of its equipment. The Town Mill Trust bought the building in 2009, linking it once again to the Town Mill. It now houses a gallery run by the Arts Guild and can be rented as a community space.

From here walk down the side of the Cheesemongers. Look through an arched

Miller's garden

window on your left to see how water from the leat is fed over the top of the waterwheel. You'll hear the clunk of the wheel if the mill is in action. The high-pitched hum is from the hydro-electric system.

Continue along the raised path known as the Lynch with the river low to your left and the higher man-made mill leat on your right. The Lynch dates back to at least 1340, when Edward III granted Lyme a licence to build a watermill 'and cause to be made a certain trench across that place to the same mill, to convey part of the river to that mill'.

A sluice gate can be seen in the wall of the leat, opposite the little bridge over the river. This controls the flow of water to the mill and should protect the area from flooding. In 2012, the leat couldn't cope with the torrent of water and debris rushing down it and the Lynch and Town Mill courtyard were flooded.

The Lynch Path

The sluice is set at the lowest point of the leat where the worst of the sludge brought down by the river accumulates. Once a year it is opened and the leat completely drained so that deposits can be shovelled away. Recently, the job of sludge-clearing has been made much easier by inviting Lyme's fire brigade over to practise their hosing skills.

The small bridge over the Lym was built in 1974 to commemorate the 1200th anniversary of the borough. Over the bridge is a little public garden with the erroneously named Leper's Well in the far wall. The Victorian name is rather misleading since this is actually a spring. From the 17th to the 19th century, a long iron gutter, known as Jones' Shoot, channelled the precious clean water across to the Lynch where it was collected by people living in this poor part of town. The plaque above the arch states that a hospital for lepers stood near this spot some 700 years ago. It is known that a lepers' hospital existed in Lyme from 1336, but nobody is sure exactly where it stood.

At the end of the Lynch, come out on to Gosling Bridge. It is easy to see how the weir controls the supply of water to the mill, channelling much of the river into the leat.

Leper's Well

A little ruined round house can be seen high up behind the weir, a relic of Lyme's cloth trade, built around 1800. Research has shown that it was used for drying fleeces around an iron stove, with a hole in the roof to let the steam out. The town manufactured woollen cloth from at least medieval times: in the 1360s, cloth was one of the main exports from the Cobb. In the 17th century, England's textile industry was centred in the West of England, and much of this cloth was brought to Lyme and shipped to France and Spain. Later, Lyme specialised in manufacturing dense, high-quality coat cloths in the small water-powered mills that lay along the River Lym. The mills employed over 200 people in 1823.

By the early 1800s, Lyme was struggling to compete with cloth produced in Yorkshire's enormous new steam-powered factories. The situation became critical when northern mills started producing cheap yarn that incorporated waste wool and rags, known as 'shoddy'. Lyme's remaining woollen factory closed in 1847.

From Gosling Bridge, proceed up Mill Green. This is still lined with about two-dozen cottages that were home to mill workers and weavers, built between 1803 and 1824 after the whole area was destroyed in a fire. Historian George Roberts wrote that the fire started in a house in George's Square on Bonfire Night (when Protestant Lyme burned an effigy of the Pope rather than Guy Fawkes). In strong winds, the sparks flew to Mill Green, destroying 42 houses and the woollen factory. Roberts remarks rather unfeelingly that, 'This accident, as it caused the destruction of many close, unhealthy houses, may be considered to have been attended with beneficial results'.

No.10 is half-way up the hill, on the left, and was the 'Factory House', the home of William Glyde who leased all the town's cloth mills.

The four-storey Old Factory once stood on the site of 1 and 2 Mill Green and stretched back to the river. It produced woollen cloth until 1843, then silk thread and was finally demolished in 1880. The arm of an old Spinning Jenny was unearthed in the garden behind the house. Surprisingly, this is the only artefact connected to Lyme's cloth industry that has ever come to light, other than the buildings themselves and a single insurance certificate.

Next door Silk Mill Cottage can be still seen on the right as the road bends left. On the far bank of the Lym was a field used for tentering – the process of fixing damp lengths of cloth onto wooden frames using tenterhooks, to prevent them from shrinking as they dried.

Continue to the end of Mill Green. Over the utilitarian concrete bridge is Jordan Flats, a three-storey cream-painted building. This was the New Factory, built between 1806 and 1824. The waterwheel stood at the far end. After the woollen mill closed, it

Jordan Flats

became a silk factory and subsequently the White Rose steam laundry. Later it was taken over by GIs preparing for D-Day, who built the flat concrete bridge to bring their jeeps over the river. The building has now been converted into flats.

To the left of the bridge is a ramp down into the river that marks the beginning of one of the longest fords in England.

Continue along the footpath to the left of the ford, cross it and continue to the junction with Woodmead Road. The weir above Woodmead Road Bridge controlled the water flow down to the New Factory. The concrete boxes in the far side of

Weir and Higher Mill

the weir act as a trout ladder to help fish migrate upstream.

This part of the Lym passes through an area that was known locally as Monkey's Rough, where the once-persecuted Baptists settled safely beyond the borough limits. Baptists first met here in 1653, immersing their converts in the river and changing out of their wet clothes in a 'dipping house' that stood on the corner of Windsor Terrace. The Baptists called this part of the river the Jordan, and many place names in this area such as Jericho, Bethel and Paradise Cottage keep the memory of these early Baptists alive.

Take Windsor Terrace until you reach Higher Mill Flats, a three-storey stone building. This has had various uses over the years: it was a linseed oil and oil cake mill up to the 1820s, a fulling mill until the woollen mills closed in 1847, and later a twine, rope and sailcloth factory. From 1909 to 1929, the mill housed a water turbine which contributed to Lyme's first electricity supply. The water wheel was at the far end of the building. When the undergrowth dies down in winter, the overflow tunnel may be seen in the river bank next to the lamppost.

Continue up Windsor Terrace towards Horn Bridge. As you approach, you can see a trough running along the right-hand side of the road. This was the leat that fed Higher Mill.

The road crossing the bridge, Colway Lane, is an old Roman branch track running between Dorchester and Exeter. This was improved in 1759 so that wheeled traffic could enter Lyme for the first time in the town's history.

On the opposite corner of the lane is Horn Tavern, an Edwardian house that stands on the site of an old fulling mill, Horn Tavern Mill. Cloth from Somerset and local mills was brought to be finished here before being sent out from the Cobb to mainland

Europe. The mill closed around 1844 when fulling was transferred downstream to Higher Mill.

Continue upstream along the narrow metalled road, following the Wessex Ridgeway. Ignore the first footbridge, and where the road bends right to Middle Mill (a farm between two mills, rather than a mill), keep left along the East Devon Way.

Cross the next footbridge over the Lym. The large weir just upstream was built to feed the leat for Horn Tavern Mill and Higher Mill. The leat would have run down the opposite side of the roadway to the present river.

Go through the gate into Bumpy Field and walk straight across the bottom of the field to another gate. This opens on to a little footbridge that crosses back over the Lym, taking you across the Dorset/ Devon border. Look out for dippers skimming the river.

In front of you is the Old Mill. This picturesque thatched watermill was reputedly built in the 14th century, though the wheel was replaced in the 1960s. The mill produced flour and bread until the early 1900s. The bakery was in the building opposite the front door.

Retrace your steps over the footbridge and decide if you want to walk back the way you've come or go uphill to a stile at the top right-hand corner of the field, then carry straight on upwards through another field, keeping the hedge to your right, until you come to a stile leading onto Haye Lane. Cross the lane and take the short footpath to the main road.

On the main road is the Old Black Dog Guesthouse and Tea Rooms. During the 17th century, an old man lived alone in Colway Manor on the outskirts of Lyme with his loyal black dog. One night, thieves broke in and demanded his hidden treasure. When the man refused them, they beat him to death, leaving the dog pining at the foot of the stairs until it finally died of starvation.

This manor house was almost completely destroyed during the Civil War, but a farmhouse was built on the site, incorporating the original fireplace and part of the roof of the old manor. Nearly every evening the farmer was joined by the ghost of a large black dog. His neighbours warned him about sharing his house with a ghost, but he said that the dog wasn't troubling anybody. However, after a few drinks one night the farmer felt that his neighbours might have a point. He rushed home, picked up a poker and chased the dog up to the attic where it vanished through the ceiling. The farmer lashed out in rage and smashed through the plaster, whereupon an ancient box fell through the hole containing a hoard of gold coins dating back to the Civil War.

The farmer used this treasure to buy a house on the corner of Haye Lane (previously called Dog Lane), converting it into a coaching inn and calling it the Black Dog after the ghostly hound. From that time, a black dog is said to haunt the area. There are records of a sighting in 1856 when a local couple spotted a small black dog approaching along the lane. As it drew nearer, the spectre grew as tall as the trees lining the lane before swelling into a huge black cloud and vanishing.

The ghostly dog was sighted by three tourists in 1959, and again in 2010 by a local man who knew nothing of the legend at the time. This man recounted how he felt a strange presence while walking his dog behind the Old Black Dog. His dog bolted into a field, and the man saw a quick dark shadow moving silently away from him towards Lyme. Local dog walkers say that their dogs are reluctant to walk along the lane and often cross to the other side as they approach the B&B.

To return to Lyme, either retrace your steps; take Haye Lane and Roman Road back to Horn Bridge (no pavement); or follow the B3165 directly back to town (pavement).

Joanna Smith has lived in Lyme Regis since 2007 after being a visitor to the town for 20 years. She has written three filmscripts that were shot in southern Africa and completed a fourth. She works as a creative writing teacher and has edited and proofed two volumes of stories written by members of her classes.

Her first book Lesser Known Lyme Regis is available from local publisher Roving Press. www.rovingpress.co.uk, tel 01300 321531.

Editor's tip: Want FREE lessons in Computing and Digital Photography?

THERE'S no better way than with Professional IT and Photography tutors – Jeffrey Oliver and Bob Shaw – Weymouth Community Volunteers, at the Digital Media Centre, 5 Gordon Row, Chapelhay, Weymouth, DT4 8LL . . . Tel: 01305 775550. Discover that, serious though these subjects are, learning about them can be fun!

HARDY ANNUAL

Mike Nixon, Secretary of the Thomas Hardy Society, reports on the year's events

EVERY year since 1968, the Thomas Hardy Society has put on various events during any given year. But every two years something special happens: Dorchester and Dorset host people from all over the world, when delegates attend the International Conference. And 2014 was one of those years. But before we look back at this major event at the end of July, it's worth reporting on what went before.

Westminster Abbey

A recent, and very welcome, innovation is the Memorial Service, held in the Abbey, marking Hardy's death on the 11th January. A simple but moving ceremony, where Hardy's poems are read and a wreath of Stinsford yew is laid on his tomb. The service this year was led by Canon Andrew Tremlett.

Folklore, Hardy and Rural Writing

An exciting first for the Society: a joint conference working with The Folklore Society. Wessex folklore, folk customs and rural traditions, and the works of Hardy formed the basis of this three day event, held at the Corn Exchange, Dorchester. In many ways this successful gathering attracted a number of new people to both organisations, and both benefited. Many speakers drew attention to the overlap in Hardy's work and the local folklore. The conference also featured a number of postgraduate papers on Hardy. The conference was professionally brought together by our Hardy Council members Dr Jacqueline Dillion and Dr Rebecca Welshman.

Hardy and Larkin

These two poets are often linked together, as it is often acknowledged that Larkin had great admiration for Hardy's work, and he did have some influence on some of his poems. At the end of March, after planning closely with the Philip Larkin Society, we all assembled at St. Anne's College, Oxford, for a joint weekend. There was unquestionably a synergy between members of each society, perhaps not surprisingly so. Lectures, readings, entertainments and walks were laid on, culminating in Poet Laureate Carol Anne Duffy reading her poetry. This was the third joint event, and we look forward to more in the future

Hardy's Birthday Weekend

This eagerly anticipated traditional event started the celebrations off with the customary walk, led by Chairman Tony Fincham. This was in countryside featured in the novel 'Far From the Madding Crowd', and centred round the Puddletown area. The Birthday lecture was delivered by our Council member Dr Rebecca Welshman, on the fascinating subject of personal archaeology and emotions in the work of Hardy. The traditional Hardy Players' contribution, showcasing their new production 'Wessex Scenes', was up to their highest standards, led by Andy Worth and Tim Laycock. The array of Dorchester Town Council councillors and aldermen and women is always a stirring sight, and much appreciated by the Society. After wreath laying at the Hardy statue, by our very own Council member and this year's mayor, Peter Mann, it was on to the William Barnes statue to lay a further wreath at the feet of this seminal Dorset poet. The evening entertainment was provided by a new group, at least in title, 'The Dorchester Bards', but was made up of very well known local people: Alistair Chisholm, Julian Nagle and Gerry Bird. Their talent did not disappoint. Sunday morning saw a church service at St Michael's, Stinsford, where Hardy's heart is buried, and a wreath was laid at the grave by Tony Fincham.

Tony Fincham laying the wreath on Hardy's grave at Stinsford

The Horse with the Red Umbrella

Yes I am talking about that uniquely named café in Dorchester! Proprietor, John Fiori has put up a prominent display which links the building with the long demolished Loyalty Theatre, actor Edmund Kean and Hardy. To mark the unveiling, John had our President, Lord Julian Fellowes and Lady Fellowes, and the Mayor of Dorchester, Peter Mann, to do the honours. A unique story.

Mayor Peter Mann, café owner John Fiori, Lord & Lady Fellowes
& Mike Nixon (photo courtesy of Dorset Echo)

The 21st Hardy Conference and Festival

As I said at the beginning of this piece, this event is always a highlight, and this year was no exception. Over 120 delegates from over a dozen different countries came to Dorchester to talk and celebrate Hardy. Over the week there were lectures, post graduate presentations, walks, coach tours, music, The New Hardy Players and a barn dance.

It is almost unfair to pick out and name names, but I have to mention just a few: Christopher Nicholson, author of 'Winter', who opened our Conference; the wonderful New Hardy Players, who just get better and better; the deservedly ubiquitous Tim Laycock who brought his massive talent to many of our events; the Beaminster Choir for a great evening and Black Sheep for providing an energetic barn dance. And to Alan Johnson MP, who talked knowledgeably and with great humour about his love of Hardy and Larkin, and not a 'political' word was uttered!

Rt Hon Alan Johnson M.P. and Mike Nixon (photo courtesy of Dorset Echo)

Dr Jane Thomas (Conference Director) with some of the overseas delegates
(photo courtesy of Dorset Echo)

But the Conference was also about ideas and theories that, particularly the many young people there, wanted to share and discuss with other post graduates. There were in addition 30+ Papers presented throughout the week, a forum for thought provoking ideas, often from people from different parts of the world, from India, France, USA, Canada, Italy, Japan and Bangladesh. There really are too many to mention, but it's what makes the Conference possible.

With such a logistical challenge, a large band of people pull out the stops all week and for weeks before that. Our thanks to all the people that helped, and special thanks must go to Dr Jane Thomas, our Conference Director, from Hull University, our retiring Chairman Tony Fincham, our Deputy, now new Chairman, Helen Lange, and of course all on the Hardy Council, without which none of this would have happened.

The London Lecture

The year came to a fitting end with our annual lecture at Birkbeck College, given this year by two of our Council members, Jacqueline Dillion and Phillip Mallett on 'Looking and Overlooking' in the 'Return of the Native'. It was an excellent and stimulating evening. Our thanks go to both speakers, and to Birkbeck who are so generous with their premises. **On to 2015 . . . .**

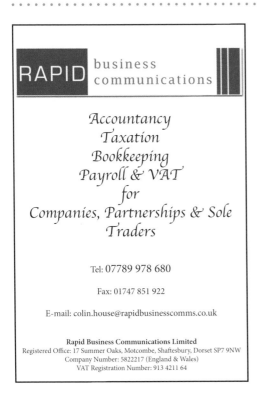

PULPIT ROCK

by Paul Snow

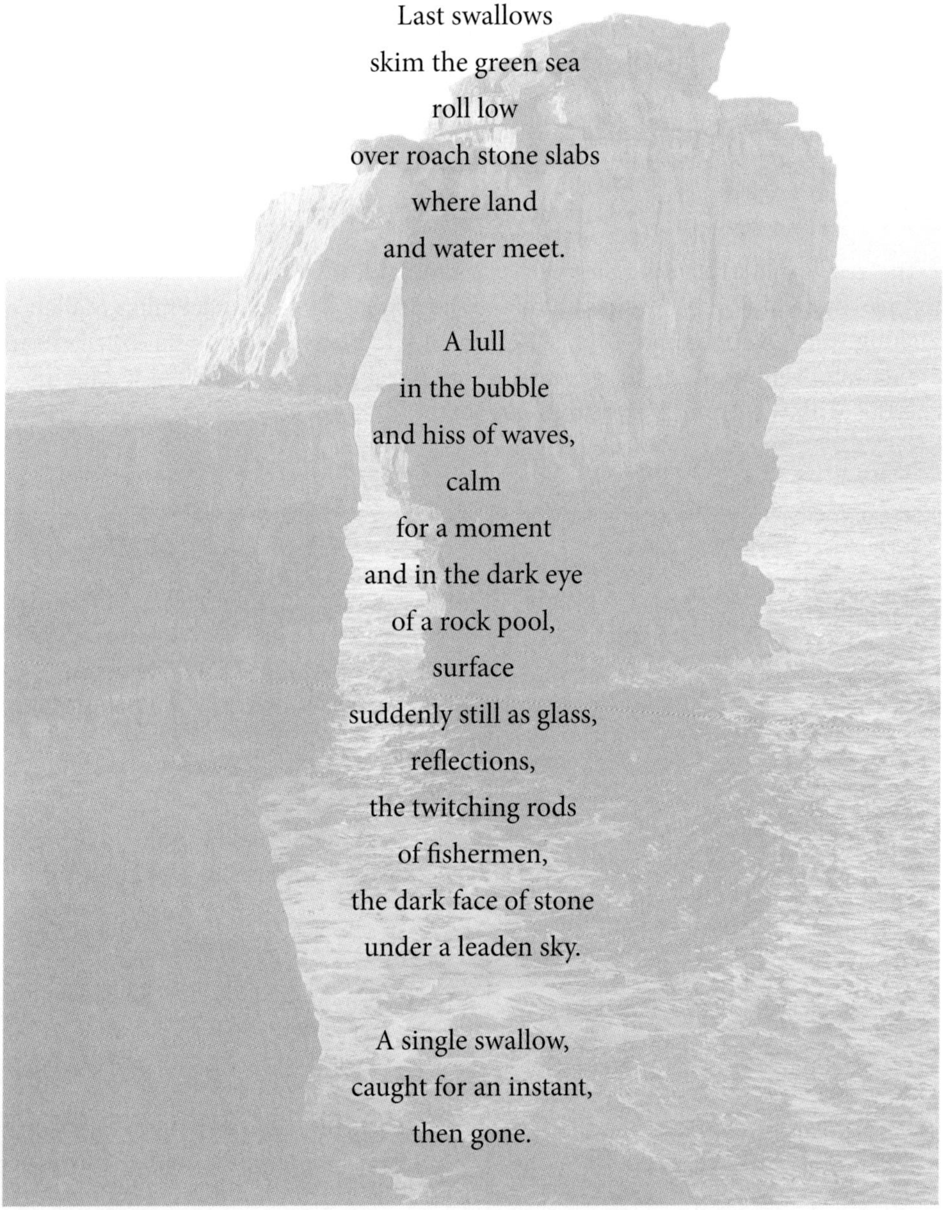

Last swallows
skim the green sea
roll low
over roach stone slabs
where land
and water meet.

A lull
in the bubble
and hiss of waves,
calm
for a moment
and in the dark eye
of a rock pool,
surface
suddenly still as glass,
reflections,
the twitching rods
of fishermen,
the dark face of stone
under a leaden sky.

A single swallow,
caught for an instant,
then gone.

WESSEX NEWFOUNDLAND SOCIETY

A brief report on the history, aims and activities to mark the 30th anniversary of the Society - by Chairman, Ian Andrews

IN 1497, John Cabot set sail in the small Bristol-built ship, "Matthew", seeking out a sea route to Cathay. In June he made a landfall on the wooded shores of a large island in the North Atlantic. Convinced he had reached Asia, he named his discovery 'New-found-land'.

The sea off the coast of Newfoundland was rich in fish, mainly cod, and, before many years had passed, every spring, intrepid fishermen from Portugal, France, and the West of England risked their lives, and their small 50 ton boats, sailing to the Grand Banks to earn rich rewards, when they returned in the autumn, selling the fish they caught in European ports.

The British, having land bases, were able to dry and salt the fish they caught on "flakes" on the shore and pack them in barrels. Other nations "split" (filleted) them on their boats and brought them back "wet," sloshing around their holds – a far more risky practice.

In Spain, Portugal and Italy the fish was in great demand by the Catholic populations. The money earned from the sale of the fish was used to buy wine, fresh and dried fruit, and goods from the Far East, like tea, which fetched high prices in England. Apart from its economic benefit, the Newfoundland fishing trade was also considered one of the best training grounds for seamen and indeed the Royal Navy press gangs targeted them. The earliest recognition of this trade in Poole records is in 1528.

In August 1583 twenty British ships were in St John's, Newfoundland, when Sir Humphrey GILBERT claimed the island for Britain as its oldest 'colony'. Once established the trade flourished. In 1594 Raleigh wrote to the Secretary of State that 100 ships were to return in August "and they must not be allowed to be captured or it would be the greatest blow ever given to England ".

In 1595 the trade revenue of the Port of Poole was over £3,000, yet seven years earlier, at the time of the Armada, if one believes the reply given, the town had been unable to furnish any ships for the defence of the realm and the Lords of the Council "being credibly informed of their dishabylyte - they are eased of this burden ".

Poole's Golden Age

By 1750, merchants of Poole had the lion's share of the trade, taking on their outward voyage the all-essential salt needed to preserve the cod, as well as food, clothing and household goods for settlers and the ropes, net, hooks and canvas needed, thus supporting the local trade economy.

Several families (the LESTERS, JEFFERYS, SPURRIERS, GARLANDS, SLADES, WHITES and JOLLIFFES) grew rich as merchants; but bearing their losses from shipwrecks and piracy without insurance as well as gains from the trade. They built the fine merchant houses that survive in Poole. Indeed Poole became the major UK port trading with Newfoundland – its Golden Age. They recruited their crews from all over a depressed agricultural Dorset and many a youngster was apprenticed "to learn the art and mystery of fishing" to take them off the parish rates.

During the latter part of the C18th and early C19th the trade suffered badly from lack of government protection of the fleets, as French and American privateers - legitimised pirates - inflicted great losses on the shipping. The dependence of the town on the trade was absolute - Poole then consisted of perhaps 5,000 persons and had produced at least one firm – SLADES - which had made a million pounds from the business.

After the Napoleonic War ended in 1815 and with American competition, trade slumped. Cod, which fetched 20/- a quintal, dropped in price to 10/-. There were bankruptcies and ruin and it took Poole many decades to recover.

The Twentieth Century

Attempts were made to revive trade in the 1920's following a visit by Lord MORRIS, Newfoundland's Premier, to Poole in 1918. It was proposed in 1924 that a trade in salt cod, transported in 200 ton vessels between May and December each year, then carried through Bristol, should transfer to Poole - but the question which defeated it was whether there was a market for the fish.

Though the discussions came to nothing, this century has seen continued contacts. The links extend to a shared place in radio history, for not only did MARCONI make his first experiments from the Haven Hotel and his yacht Elettra, but it was to St John's that he sent the world's first trans-ocean signals from Poldhu in Cornwall. Another modern link is the shared interest in oil - at Wytch Farm and the offshore field under Poole Bay and from the Hibernia project off the shores of the Province.

Jump to the 1980's and the efforts of a number of people to re-establish links. In Newfoundland, Otto Tucker and Cyril Poole of the Memorial Unversity of Newfoundland, teamed up. As Otto says "I began seriously a lifetime crusade "in search of" what author Cyril Poole calls "the Newfoundland soul."

That search took a significant turn in 1984 when a group from Newfoundland founded the Wessex Society of Newfoundland to disseminate information about Newfoundland's roots in the West Country of England. Otto writes, "The search also took me on nostalgic and research visits to the West Country; and special is that day in 1983 when I met Alan Perry and his wife Jill in their wine shop on the Poole quay." The Canadian Broadcasting Company's outstanding daily programme was "Land and Sea" and they sent their chief presenter, David Quinton (who has New Forest ancestors) to film. The late Peter Coles, former Mayor of Poole, and the town's Chief Executive (the writer) had also visited the province.

The foundation of a Wessex Society in Newfoundland in 1984 and, after a public meeting, of the Wessex Newfoundland Society in England in 1985 has done much to remind people of the centuries-long links and to bring today's peoples together in close bonds of friendship and common heritage. Three out of four of Newfoundland's inhabitants can trace their ancestry to the West Country. Even so, in 1949, a narrow majority of 51 % to 49% voted to join Canada as its newest Province, but this could not obliterate the obvious remains of dialect and phrases - "Where be ye to?" - still to be heard.

And Today. . .

The Wessex Newfoundland Society fosters links between the people of Poole and Dorset and the surrounding areas of Wessex and those of Newfoundland and Labrador.

Its aims and objects are:-

* To broaden the mutual understanding of the historical, cultural, educational, recreational, civic and commercial activities of the linked areas by the exchange of information and development of personal contacts:

* To enable those with this interest to come together in a context that would satisfy their need:

* To promote, support or subscribe to such activities or organisations as may further the aims of the Society and carry out such activities as are necessary to further these aims.

Wessex Newfoundland Society membership is not confined to the West Country. Members have come from not only all over Britain, having a variety of interests (by birth, descent, employment or historical interest), but also from Newfoundland, mainland Canada and the US – and even Australia.

The Borough of Poole and the City of St John's have joined in a Declaration of Friendship. One of the two Universities in Poole (Bournemouth) has been twinned with Memorial University in St John's (MUN), and scholarships established for a number of its students to study in St John's.

Talks are arranged in Poole which attract a wide attendance and although it is not a family history society as such, it works closely with Dorset FHS. Visitors have included Lieutenant Governors and a Premier. The Society has also organised several conducted group tours, including a Lord Lieutenant of the County and local MP's, to the Province, at which we have received splendid receptions. We were present when the replica "Matthew" sailed into Bonavista on Cabot's anniversary, to be received by HM The Queen and Prince Philip (and a guard of honour of 100 Newfoundland dogs!). (The Matthew replica is now docked in Bristol).

Composed from members, Trinity Trust (a charity registered in the UK and Canada) was formed to restore the derelict Lester Garland House in Trinity (only two gable walls were then still standing). The original was built in 1761 from Dorset bricks and with window glass shipped out in the C18th. A target of $2m (Can) was set and ultimately met and rebuilding achieved in a country of wooden houses with the help of restoration expertise from Bournemouth University. It is probably the oldest surviving brick-built house in North America and is used as a museum and education centre to rekindle, promote and celebrate the strong historical and cultural links between Newfoundland and the west of England, especially those between Trinity and Dorset.

We were also present when the settlement at Cupids was 400 years old. From there we saw the largest ever Union Flag flown. Union flags are still very common and proudly flown from houses.

A colourful dawn view of downtown St John's from Signal Hill

A recent copy of The Link

The Link

The one thing that unites all members, wherever they live, is the quarterly 60-page magazine ("The Link") that was edited and printed by Peter Coles for the first 39 issues, until his death. Subsequent issues have been compiled and published by me. The December 2014 issue is no. 99! We reproduce relevant material of News from Newfoundland and News from the UK, as well as featuring historical research and leading articles, book and other reviews. For further information and to join, contact our Hon Treasurer, Brian J. Galpin on 01202-672038.

Alan Perry, my predecessor as Chairman, has been rightly rewarded for making over 60 trips to the province by an honorary Doctorate, an OBE in the Commonwealth list and an ONL, Canada's highest honour. I believe Alan to be the only 'foreigner' ever to receive the latter.

In 1901, the Morning Post of London wrote (and it is still true):-

"The Newfoundlanders are wholly Anglo-Saxon and Celtic stock, and nowhere in the Colonies is there a population more British in their appearance, manners and sentiment.

Living in this climate, so similar to our own, the people have the fresh complexion of our own West Country men and the hardy look of our deep-sea fishermen.

Newfoundland has ever kept itself closer in touch with the Old Country than with the mainland of America. It is an island in which the Englishman soon finds himself at home, and he cannot fail to love these people among whose leading characteristics are an unaffected heartiness, kindliness and hospitality."

A replica of 'Matthew'

Dorset County Museum – History and Future

An appraisal by Museum Marketing Manager – Rachel Cole

The Dorset County Museum

DORSET County Museum is an independent museum owned and managed by the Dorset Natural History and Archaeological Society. It also receives some financial support from Dorset County Council and West Dorset District Council.

The mission of the Museum today is the advancement of education for the general benefit of the public in the areas of archaeology, the natural sciences, natural history, literature, music, the fine and decorative arts, antiquities and local history relating to the County of Dorset.

In addition it is committed to the acquisition, preservation, conservation, exhibition and development of collections relating to these areas.

Brief History

The Museum was established in 1846 to save the natural history and archaeology of a county at risk from the effects of the Industrial Revolution. The coming of the railways in the 1840s saw Dorchester's Roman heritage threatened with destruction – Isambard Kingdom Brunel's proposal was to drive a railway line right through Poundbury Hill Fort and Maumbury Rings!

The poet, William Barnes, and the vicar of Fordington, the Reverend Henry Moule, decided to form an organisation that would protect these sites and the natural history of the area. On 1 July 1846 the Dorset County Museum and Library was founded. It successfully persuaded the railway company to change its route, and provided a home for archaeological and natural history finds from around the county. The original museum was founded in the building where the 'bloody assizes' took place following the Monmouth Rebellion – now the Prezzo restaurant.

By the 1860s the museum had moved first to Trinity Street and later to the site of the Old George Inn, a former public house on High West Street. It was even housed for a while at Sherborne. This lack of permanent accommodation meant that the Museum suffered from a lack of space and could only open on Thursdays and Saturdays. The visitor numbers were so low as a consequence that, when the Society attempted to recruit a curator in the 1870s they could not persuade anyone to take on the role!

Victorian Gallery

To try to rectify the situation, a public subscription was launched, headed by the Prince of Wales. Supported by the clergy and the gentry, the fund raised enough money to employ architect CR Crickmay to design the present building in High West Street, and it was opened by the father of British Archaeology, General Pitt-Rivers, in 1883.

Although some visitors think it looks like a church, the height of the original design provided aesthetics and grandeur and, in a street of other high buildings, a good deal of natural light. The rose window in particular allowed the sunlight to flood in whilst obscuring views of the prison, situated directly behind!

The first Curator

In the new gothic museum, Henry Joseph Moule, son of the Rev Henry Moule, was appointed as the first full-time curator. He quickly set about classifying, arranging and supervising the collections and corresponded widely with other specialists.

He also fundraised in order to build additional galleries and at the time of his death in 1904 was still arranging the new displays.

Moule's lasting legacy was an astonishing collection of several thousand watercolours which he painted as a result of his daily walks around the countryside. His sketches are a unique record of Victorian Dorset and they strongly evoke the Wessex of Thomas Hardy's books.

Mosaic

Expansion and Awards

In 1937 the Dorset County Education Committee gave a grant to the Museum to encourage it to build links with local schools. A new Geology Gallery opened the same year, and in 1938 Thomas Hardy's papers and the contents of his Max Gate study were bequeathed to the Museum.

Following the Second World War, while other museums were struggling, Dorset's growing tourist industry meant that the Museum was able to expand. A new Natural History Gallery was built in 1952 and a new Archaeology Gallery completed in 1984, earning Dorset County Museum a prestigious National Heritage Museum of the Year award.

With the advent of Heritage Lottery Funding since the 1990s, many galleries have been added and refurbished. The Writers' Dorset Gallery opened in 1997, winning a further Museum of the Year award, while the Dorchester Gallery opened in 2003 and the Jurassic Coast Gallery in 2006.

Challenges and benefits to Society

Today Dorset County Museum is faced with a whole new set of challenges and opportunities.

We all know that the UK has a lot of museums – today there are anywhere between 1800 and 2500 depending on how you define them. In the past museums were largely autonomous – today they must justify their decisions to the government, to their audiences, funders and a whole range of stakeholders. The main challenge is how to reach out to new audiences and find ways of communicating with them. The rewards are many – to maintain status and respect, to win hearts and influence people, and to foster a sense of community, identity and even nationhood.

How successfully is Dorset County Museum dealing with these challenges?

We have to look at what the British Museums Association definition of a museum is –

Fossilised Fish

'Museums enable people to explore collections for inspiration, learning and enjoyment. They are institutions that collect, safeguard and make accessible artefacts and specimens, which they hold in trust for the benefit of society.'

This rightly puts objects at the centre of the museum's primary function, but the social dimension is also important – that collections are held in trust for the benefit of society.

In recent years new approaches have increasingly been taken within museums which point towards a changing and enhanced role for museums within the wider community. These changes can be grouped into the areas of Collecting, Exhibiting, Promotion, Advocacy and Partnership, Learning and Social Change.

Collecting

Dorset County Museum continues to develop and expand its collections.

This takes the form of development and improvement of the museum galleries, the acquisition of new objects and treasure, and working with partners to display

Moving the pliosaur - with the Army to help

and interpret new objects such as the Weymouth Bay Pliosaur and the Hardy Players manuscripts.

One area in which the nature of collecting has significantly changed in recent years is that of Social History. In the past many collections, if not most, were assembled by an elite group which wished to improve the rest of society. Since the 1970s and the advent of social history in our field, museums have put much more effort into collecting the ordinary and everyday, in recognition of the fact that it is this material which best represents the lives of the majority of the population. This has an academic underpinning, as well as bringing the additional benefit of enabling museums to show their relevance to people who previously were underrepresented, and perhaps therefore uninterested in museum displays.

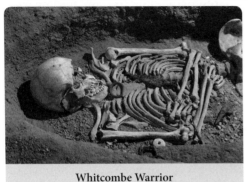
Whitcombe Warrior

Moreover, museums which collect social history tend to have forged further links with audiences through their movement into contemporary collecting and community curatorship – a field neglected by historians in museums for so long that the 20th century was at some risk of almost being bypassed altogether.

Exhibiting

There have been a number of shifts in exhibiting, many of them controversial. Much of this criticism seems to stem from the use of technology in order to breathe more life into certain subjects. Exhibition design and presentation techniques can excite revulsion, especially where interactivity, sound or lighting effects, or film are employed, presumably because all these interpretative techniques are alleged to detract from the serious issues represented by objects.

At Dorset County Museum few of these techniques are used because of limited budgets, but we have strived to raise our game by working with national institutions like the National Portrait Gallery, National Museums Liverpool and the British Museum to improve the quality of our own exhibitions and bring world class touring shows to Dorset, such as the Pharaoh: King of Egypt exhibition from the British Museum in 2011.

We try to recognise that there is no 'right' way to create museum displays, object-rich or not, and that everyone's response to displays is different. Making exhibitions which are wide-ranging in content and relevant to contemporary society is fundamental to building the broader audiences modern museums need, and ought to be serving, in all their diversity. Ultimately, objects rarely 'speak for themselves'. They can be the spark that lights the blue touch paper of wonder, awe, emotion or a host of other reactions, intellectual or visceral, but we must present the rest of the story too, and if some parts of the story cannot be told using objects, we must find other ways of doing it.

Promotion

In the past Museums did not generally have 'marketing departments'. Exhibition posters and other publicity material were cobbled together by curators and volunteers and this lack of professionalism was typical of the low priority given to museum audiences.

No wonder the traditional museum appealed only to a minority of the population when it was such a well-kept secret!

Nor, of course, did museums know much about their audiences; who used the museums and who didn't, and why. The modus operandi was to carry on knocking out temporary exhibitions and adding the occasional permanent display, almost through force of habit, rather than because they were trying to identify and match audience needs or interests.

As museums have increasingly had to work harder to protect their funding, they have had no choice but to find out more about their audiences, to try to understand motivation for visiting, and lack of motivation for not visiting, and to establish sustainable contact. Today our larger museums invest large sums in audience research to inform decisions about how to market and promote their events, exhibitions and activities.

One of the most important tools in building new audiences is by harnessing the power of the local media. These media are on our doorstep, hungry for editorial content, and they are read, watched or listened to by all the people we want to attract to our museums. Forging an effective relationship with these media is just as central to the fortunes of any museum that wishes to develop its audiences as its exhibition and events programme. Dorset County Museum has worked hard to improve the effectiveness of its communication with the local press, radio and TV agencies – it was heavily involved in Radio Four's History of the World project which resulted in much closer links with local TV companies.

Advocacy and Partnership

These terms can be used to summarise the huge network of relationships the modern museum needs to establish in order to maximise its effectiveness. It is no longer an option to remain isolated and aloof. Museums are social organisations,

Hands Up - A School visit

and can be powerful – they need to assume their rightful place in the mainstream of contemporary life, not sit eccentrically on the margins.

This means networking with, and advocating our value to, other sectors of society. Some of these are traditional allies of museums – such as the higher education sector – others have been more remote, such as the political, business and community sectors.

Many museums are now extremely good at political lobbying. Some have successful business clubs, vehicles to involve and inform the business community about the value of museums in making places better to live and work in. Others have developed partnerships with scores of agencies including social services, health and youth services, disability agencies, libraries, environmental agencies, special schools, organisations representing ethnic or minority groups and a whole host of others. Often such partnerships involve active consultation by museums with interest groups which can advise them in areas where they are short on expertise. Dorset County Museum, for example, regularly works with a wide range of organisations including the National Trust, Thomas Hardye School, the Jurassic Coast Team, local councils and other cultural bodies. This results in engagement with people who have different kinds of knowledge, insights and wisdom, to the benefit of all.

Learning

Museums have always dealt in learning. This is clear from any number of stories about the motivations of those who founded so many museums in the 19th century. The recent shift, however, has been from passive learning to active learning as museums have, albeit belatedly, given more authority and responsibility to education professionals and moved from instruction to involvement.

Museum Makers - using scissors

Museums have recognised that we cannot rely on traditional exhibition techniques to reach out and impact on broad audiences. We need to rethink our methods completely so that the expertise of our curators is unlocked, and so that we can move out of our traditional, object-centred comfort zones.

Museum makers -
Skeleton Activity

We need to find new connections, new languages, new techniques and, most of all, new attitudes if we are to broaden our relevance and our scope, placing education and learning at the very centre of what we do.

Dorset County Museum's mission is based upon learning. It has created a staffing structure that puts learning in the front line, integrating it with all other functions; it encourages a culture of learning by promoting teamwork and overcoming the traditional elevation of the curator to a position superior to that of other staff. It takes positive action to include people traditionally excluded from museums by dealing with issues of relevance to them, and it acknowledges that people have different needs and different ways of learning. It has devised leaning programmes to suit its varied audiences and seeks to provide ever-increasing access to the public.

Social Change

Museums can play a very real part in changing people's lives. Dorset County Museum aims to do this primarily through the promotion of learning and raising educational aspiration. One example of this is through our work with groups of people who, traditionally, did not visit museums. Every week since the beginning of 2011, adults with learning difficulties come to the Museum from Douglas Jackman House in Dorchester. They do a wide range of activities, from creative crafts to film-making – they have also put on plays and curated their own exhibition. The effects on some of the people involved have been considerable – one young woman who had not left the home voluntarily in over three years now comes happily to the Museum and joins in with every session.

Roman helmet and ipad - School visit

Many of these schemes involve small numbers of people. As long as programmes are sustained over a long period, however, it is perfectly possible for museums to make a real difference in the community and projects which have humble beginnings can ultimately be the foundation for large scale impact. In this we begin to see the ultimate value of museums – to promote social change through learning, using our collections where appropriate but not regarding them as an end in themselves. The traditional role of museums has begun to be redefined and their social and educational value demonstrated more than ever before. This, then, is why museums are ultimately worth having in the first place.

Explore the future

These are some of the issues and debates concerning the modern museum and its changing role in society. Not all museums are the same, so it is dangerous to generalise, but in their variety lies one of their greatest strengths.

In the future museums will continue to face many challenges – they are not immune from the realities of the commercial world. Some will argue that when reductions in public spending are required, museums are not essential. This is clearly not the case – museums can explore stories that no one else will or can. People will want to continue to visit museums as long as those museums actively want to attract them. Our collections, used imaginatively to help unlock understanding and enjoyment, will never lose their power.

The launch of the Society's display case in the Hardy gallery

A Notorious Rogue

Jack Sweet makes no claim to being related . . . .but what devilish escapades !

MY great great grandmother, Susan Hanham (also spelt Hannam) was born in Hilton in 1821 the daughter of Thomas and Lydia Hanham, and during my research into the family I chanced across the story of one, Richard Hannam, who by any standards could be classed as a 'notorious rogue, if not a 'master criminal'. And here is his story.

Richard Hannam was born in Shaftesbury some time in the first half of the 17th century, the son of a shoemaker. He was packed off to London to become an apprentice silk weaver but did not remain long at the trade and settled for the more convivial occupation of a tapster. It soon appeared, however, that the life of drawing beer in an alehouse was not to Richard's liking, perhaps it lacked excitement or the money was poor, because the lad from Shaftesbury joined a gang of burglars and became quite notorious in his new found trade.

It was remarked, however, that his exploits were not accompanied by violence, which was unusual for the time and therefore found worthy of comment.

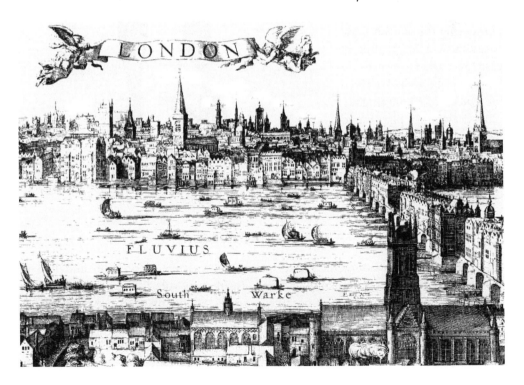

Using his talents in this line of business, Richard Hannam moved up into the realms of the aristocracy - perhaps a step too far - and he was caught stealing plate from the Earl of Pembroke. However our resourceful Richard escaped, and fled the country; a sensible course of action.

A scoundrel in Scandinavia

During his sojourn across the English Channel, Richard travelled through various countries living on his wits and finally arrived in Denmark where his fertile mind conceived a scheme which would put robbing an earl into the shadows!

Our man from Dorset settled for nothing less than plundering the Danish royal treasury of a large sum of cash and then onwards to Sweden where he relieved the Queen of £4000 in gold, plus valuable plate and jewellery.

Naturally, depredations on this scale could not be ignored and Richard found himself behind bars and not long for this world.

A rotter in Rotterdam

Once more our resourceful rogue managed to escape retribution and fled to Rotterdam where he set up as a merchant. In his new role Richard soon gained a reputation for fair dealing and became a respected member of the community; however, he was only waiting for the right opportunity. . . and when it came he decamped across the North Sea, with a large sum of money entrusted to him for 'safekeeping' by fellow merchants, and settled in London.

No boundaries for a bounder

This time his reputation had followed him, and Richard Hannam was forced to flee the country with Paris as his destination. His presence in the French capital was short lived and our notorious rogue was arrested and thrown into gaol. Once again bars could not hold him and making his escape, he returned to London.

The year was 1654 and remarkably, bearing in mind his previous activities in the city, Richard lived for some time in a grand style until funds began to run low. The burglary of a City Alderman's house in Fleet Street was a disaster. Richard escaped, but his three companions - two men and a women - were caught, convicted and quickly hanged.

Richard Hannam's freedom was short lived and he was taken, tried and sentenced to death. The trial was held on a Saturday and he was sentenced to be hanged on the following Monday. Once again his quick wits saved his life and by turning King's evidence against some thieves who had robbed the French Ambassador, he gained a stay of execution and made his escape.

The Rapscallion finally takes the Rap

Remaining at large and no doubt back in the criminal underworld, Richard took to forging the coinage of the realm - but time and luck were running out. In 1656 in company with his father-in-law, he robbed an alehouse keeper, but his partner was arrested on the evidence of the victim. In what appears to have been an uncharacteristic action, possibly egged on by his wife, Richard sought out the innkeeper and stabbed him in revenge for the capture of his relative. He was taken, tried, found guilty and this time there would be no escape. Richard Hannam, after confessing his past sins, was hanged at Smithfield on Tuesday 17 June 1656.

(Researched from the Dictionary of National Biography 1885-1900 Volume 2)

The Editor's recommendation:

Exploration of Dorset through the Internet

Look at things a little differently, read behind-the-scenes perspectives, and enjoy updates on literary and Dorset events and people.

If you like exploring our County – even from an armchair – check out Roving Press on Facebook, Twitter, Pinterest and Blogger via links at www.rovingpress. co.uk – You won't be disappointed.

A Celebrated Artist who loved Dorset

Arthur Cecil Fare (1876-1958) was both an acclaimed artist and architect in his own lifetime, associated mainly with Bath, Bristol and London.

FEW realise his links with Dorset but through family connections he grew to love our County.

His niece was the actress Ethel Fare who achieved personal success as the lead in the 1922 production of Hardy's play A Desperate Remedy when standing in for her former school friend Gertrude Bugler of The Hardy Players, who had to pull out of the role when falling pregnant. The national press described Ethel as "a brilliant newcomer".

His brother was Wilfred J Fare, Mayor of Dorchester in 1931, and his nephew Rex was a Dorset County Councillor.

Arthur spent many holidays and long periods of retirement after the second world war with his great niece Annette and her husband, our Fellow Dorset John Travell, in Dorchester.

Arthur Cecil Fare

His works on Dorset, as illustrated within this article, speak for themselves of a man of great artistic and architectural talent and skill. Most have never been reproduced before or given public exposure.

International jazz musician, song writer, recording artist, composer of film scores and art lover Andy Leggett takes up the story of A C Fare RWA FRIBA and recalls.

One afternoon in the early seventies I spent my last six pounds in a junk shop on a stunning watercolour of Granville, Normandy signed A C Fare RWA. I had to find out more . . . .

Arthur Cecil Fare was an architect practising in Bristol and Bath but is better known today for his lively watercolours of mainly architectural subjects throughout Dorset and the West Country, in London and much of Europe.

The youngest of four brothers, he was born in Bath and educated there, although he very nearly failed to get that far. A domestic gas explosion had one day blown the infant Arthur up the garden in his pram and broken his mother's ankles. He was unhurt however and later, at the age of five, held a toy trumpet while his photograph was taken by William Friese-Greene, the English pioneer of the motion-picture, at no.7 The Corridor, Bath. Forty five years later, Fare was to design the memorial plaque for those premises.

As a young man he was keen on tennis, swimming and chess and became proficient on the cello. He sold his first picture at the age of 16 - of an old house on the outskirts of Bath – to the lady occupier who was happy to pay him half-a-crown, some carrots, onions and a marrow.

One day, during his first job in an architect's office, his boss took him by the ear to admire a framed reproduction of the famous "Fifty years of Architecture" drawing by T E Brewer, commissioned in 1892 to celebrate the golden jubilee of the respected journal, The Builder. "Now Fare," he asked "Do you think you will ever be able to make a drawing like that?" This question turned out to be a self-fulfilling prophesy as Fare's own drawing "Fifty years of Architecture 1892-1942" duly appeared in The Builder on January 1st 1943 and was later exhibited at the Royal Academy.

Fare was commissioned to do drawings of the Piccadilly Hotel and Regent Street for architect Norman Shaw and a series of monumental drawings of London for other clients. These included the new Waterloo Bridge for The Builder and perspective drawings for Lutyens' scheme for the layout of the Trafalgar Square fountains and sculptures.

Arthur Fare survived the 1914-18 war performing clerical work in the army. Being short, bespectacled and somewhat shy and reticent, he described himself as "the world's worst soldier." With the hostilities over, he moved to Clifton, as a lecturer for organised courses for ex-servicemen at the Bristol School of Architects.

In 1919 he was elected to membership of "The Savages" – the Bristolian society of artists, famous for its two hour sessions for sketching and painting on Wednesday evenings. Reginald P Way, in his autobiography Antique Dealer, records when he was invited as a guest. His host rushed from the artist's room to declare "the new chap from Bath has paralysed them; his picture will be the one on the easel of honour tonight and it's wonderful." The subject was Procession and he wrote: "A. C. Fare had chosen a religious procession in a continental town; the left of the sketch was taken up by the great open door of the cathedral from which came a procession of priests, acolytes and other ecclesiastical figures carrying crosses, candles and banners. The fine detail work of the cathedral and the old houses in the streets were most beautifully drawn and the figures in the procession were truly marvellous considering the whole thing had been painted in two hours." In 1927 Fare was elected President of Bristol Savages.

Arthur Cecil Fare was prolific. He provided pen-and-ink drawings to illustrate books and magazines, his paintings were reproduced as Christmas cards and Sir

Pencil drawing of Corfe Castle

Winston Churchill, on his 80th birthday, was the lucky recipient of a Fare work. He meticulously made a postage-stamp-sized painting which was accepted for Queen Mary's famous dolls' house. Between 1922 and 1956 A C Fare exhibited well over 100 paintings at the Royal West of England Academy.

An aspect of Fare's work for which he deserves special recognition was his ability to produce realistic, atmospheric paintings of long-lost buildings which he could have known only from small-sized or otherwise inadequate prints.

In the years between the wars, Fare would take painting holidays in either Dorset or on mainland Europe . . . by public transport. He would sometimes sell the paintings, still wet from the easel, to fascinated spectators.

Although Fare was a partner in several architect's practices he was never enthusiastic as an architect. One colleague said he was a very nervous little man who used to hide behind his door when clients were announced so that it appeared he was out of the office. His work was always in demand and during this period he designed the Bath Fire Station.

Although Arthur Fare was married – his wife Marie Josephine played the piano – they never had any children.

The Second World War must have been a harrowing time for him. On the night of Sunday 24th November 1940 he was watching from the high back windows of his home as the Luftwaffe pounded the centre of Bristol to rubble. The oil painting he created, as the bombs fell and shortly after, shows the city landmarks all silhouetted against a wall of flame lighting up a smoke-filled sky. The painting is of an impressive size and was bought by Bristol Art Gallery, reproduced in colour and sold at two-and-sixpence a print.

As more of the city was ruined Fare took to painting the remains of the devastated buildings. It was almost as though he was saying goodbye to old friends. With his near-photographic memory Fare was able to produce some really beautiful paintings of some of the buildings which had been lost.

In the aftermath of the war Fare was busily involved in the plans for rebuilding the bomb-damaged City of Bath. An impressive book published in 1945 entitled "A Plan for Bath" is copiously illustrated with A C Fare drawings of "what might have been".

Arthur Fare had an uneasy relationship with the automobile. Not only did cars tend to sit slightly awkwardly in some of his architectural drawings where their presence was required; in real life he apparently drove a green Morris Minor with the opposite of panache. He is said to have deliberately kept the "Running in – Please pass" notice in the rear window long after it ceased to apply.

Around 1950 it seems that Arthur Fare contributed to Sir Giles Gilbert Scott's rebuilding of the bomb-damaged roof of the London Guildhall. A print exists reproducing his fine painting of that interior.

Arthur's wife Marie, who had never appeared to be the picture of health, died in March 1955.

Fare survived her by three years, still painting busily. Following a fall he was taken to hospital and was seen painting at his bedside until shortly before his death on 7th October 1958.

Athelhampton House

Milton Abbas

Christcurch Priory

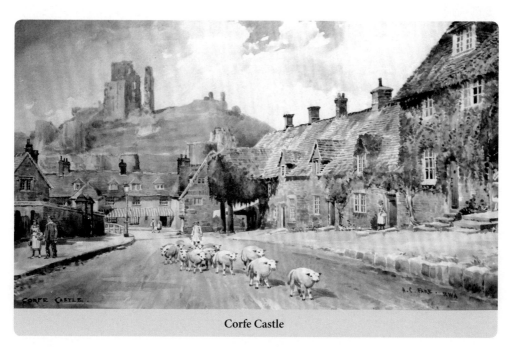

Corfe Castle

Hammoon Manor

Poxwell Manor

Another View of Athelhampton House

Milton Abbey

RUPERT CHAWTON BROOKE (1887 – 1915)

remembered 100 years on. . .

HIS tragic death on St. George's Day in 1915, caused by blood poisoning from a mosquito bite on the Greek island of Skyros, stands as a symbol of the wasted youth of a 'lost generation' through the First World War.

Rupert Brooke spent holidays at Bournemouth and Lulworth, which he described as "the most beautiful village in England". On one visit, whilst boating, he dropped his copy of Keats into the water. He immediately leapt overboard to retrieve it, probably not realising that it was from this same place that John Keats left England forever; being destined to die in Rome of tuberculosis in 1821.

After securing a commission with the Royal Naval Division at the outbreak of war, it was during training at Blandford Camp that Sub-Lieutenant R. C. Brooke wrote perhaps his best known poem and in so doing provided his own sad epitaph.

If I should die, think only this of me:

That there's some corner of a foreign field

that is for ever England.

There shall be in that rich earth a richer dust concealed;

a dust whom England bore, shaped, made aware,

gave once her flowers to love, her ways to roam,

a body of England's, breathing English air,

washed by the rivers, blest by suns of home.

(inspired by 'Reflections and Dorset Recollections' – 1995 - by the late Maurice S. Ennals)

COPYRIGHT DISCLAIMER

Short Par Three

by Terry "Life's a [golf] Ball" Herbert

So I'm placed upon the tee

looking at a short par three

A drop shot he can ill afford

with name well down the Leader Board

He feels he's hit me straight and true

convinced he'll make a Birdie two

sailing sweetly to the flag

taking putter from his bag

Yes – he thinks he's in control

steering me towards the hole

but I have got the upper hand

that's why I'm heading for the sand

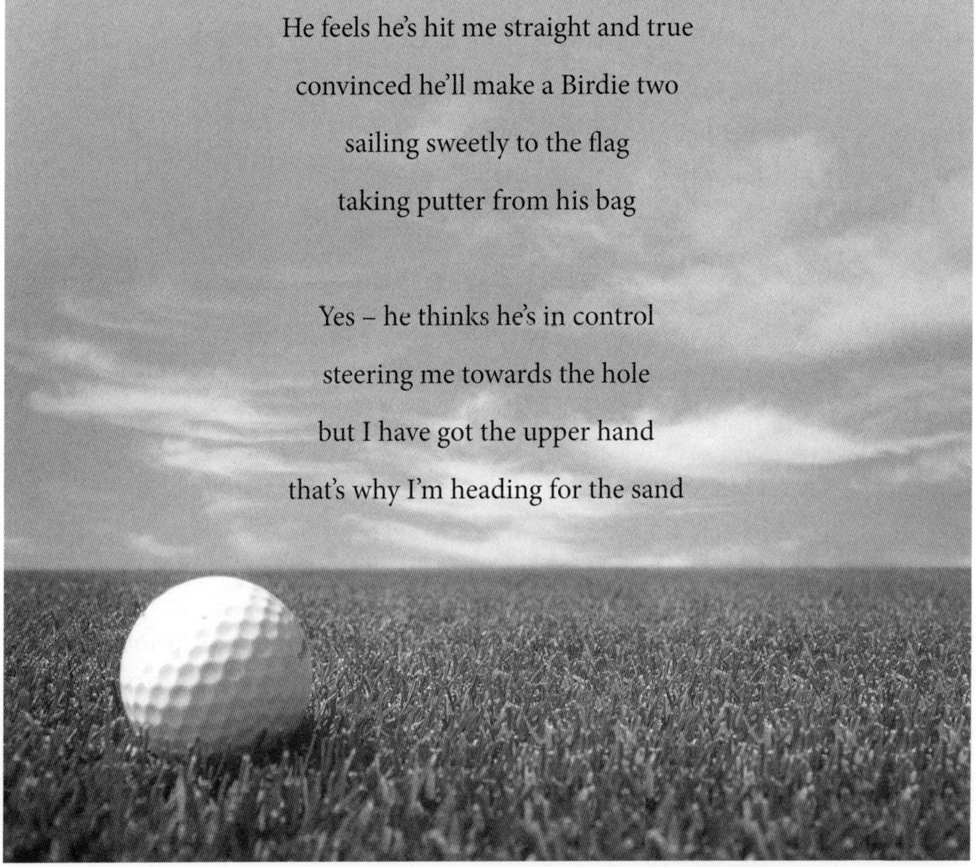

A bunker shot and here I lay

On the green, but far away

A hole in one would win the car

Now he has to make his Par

So he sizes up his shot

Left to right, or maybe not

Right to left, that's for sure

God forbid a Bogey four

No matter what his caddie said

I'm struck and yet I'm still not dead

For fate and fortune rest with me

Hence a five on Short Par Three

From Weymouth to Wazir Akbar Khãn

An Afghan Journey by Nick Carter OBE

'If we don't end war, war will end us.' H G Wells

WHEN I started my Ministry of Defence (MOD) Career as a 17 year old Engineering Apprentice at the Admiralty Underwater Weapons Establishment (AUWE), Portland, I did not think that some 30 years later I would spend nearly two years advising the Senior Leadership of the Afghan Ministry of Defence.

I was born and brought up in Weymouth and Portland and with all the Defence related activity in the area, mostly supporting the Royal Navy, there was always a good chance that I might end up working in Her Majesty's Service. This I did.

How my mission in Afghanistan came about was rather accidental. For some five years I took Advisor Training in support of numerous UK Armed Forces Exercises with a view to become a Policy Advisor with one of the UK Military Operations around the world. This was pretty tough as I was at that time heading up a joint Civilian / Military Team assessing the Logistics Performance for Current Operations and advising on Future Operations. Back in April 2012, I was about to take my name off the list of Policy Advisors available for operations when I had a phone call from the Head of the Afghan Operations Directorate asking me to go, as quickly as possible, to Kabul as an Advisor to the Afghan Minister of National Defence (MinDef); at that time General Abdul Rahim Wardak.

The current advisor had been there for nearly 2 years and it was now time for him to come home. After medicals, drawing kit and completing pre-deployment training I was ready to go on 26 May 2012. I arrived in RAF Brize Norton at midnight for the first leg of my 4,500 mile journey, leaving behind my wife Irene and sons Milo and Owain. A seven hour flight to Al Minhad Air Base in the United Arab Emirate, then a wait in very hot and humid conditions for a two and a half hour flight to the biggest coalition base in the country, Camp Bastion, approximately the size of Reading!

The plane was cramped with every seat full and after an adrenaline ride, some 24 hours after leaving the UK, I arrived at 0200 hours with the heat still 20°C and rising.

As an MOD Civilian the kit provided was minimal, but with winter temperatures that can potentially drop down to -20°C , some good cold weather gear was necessary, even though, on arrival, I did seriously wonder why I had it in my bag!

I was in Bastion five days; time enough to complete my 'in theatre' Reception, Staging and Onward Integration (RSOI), which consisted of everything as per my military colleagues except Weapons Training and Drills; UK Civil Servants are not permitted to carry or use any weapons. I found the physical challenges, including the marches, straight forward and as a member of St John Ambulance, the emergency aid training was interesting. Always carrying morphine injectors and tourniquets brought home the seriousness of the situation and the fact that I was working in a war zone.

During the day the temperature was up to 40°C so huge pallets of bottled water and supplies of insect repellent and suntan lotion were all around the camp, the essentials for life in Afghanistan.

Life in Kabul – Work, Rest and Play

The flight to Kabul took about one and a half hours followed by a 20 minute ride, with a close protection team, through a dark and silent City to the Diplomatic Quarter located in The Green (Protected) Zone. The British Embassy Kabul (BEK), in the Wazir Akbar Khān neighbourhood, was to be my home and part time place of work.

The vision of splendour and grandeur of the Embassy all ended when the Soviets left in 1989 and civil war ensued. The original 1919 British Building ended up under the control of Pakistan. When the Taliban fell in 2001, we ended up renting land and facilities from the Bulgarians - real diplomacy in action! I was lucky, for the next two years, to have a 'Pod' at the Embassy; my own self-contained and compact, sleeping, washing and living area.

Whilst living at the British Embassy, my main place of work was the Afghan MOD; far from luxurious and a mix of Soviet Style Block Architecture and local structures - functional,except for the toilets.

Security was paramount. There were at least three security staff for every diplomat in Afghanistan and, apart from the Ambassador who had Royal Military Police Protection, everybody was an employee of a private security company. Kabul, like the rest of Afghanistan, was treated as a war zone. I can only recall three weeks when I didn't hear bombs, bullets or rocket propelled grenades (RPGs) going off. Travel was terrible with cars travelling at speed in all directions on the same roads as donkey carts. Everybody, except me, carried an assortment of weapons. Getting the job done was always tricky.

My first day at the MOD proved to be one that would set the scene for the rest of my time there. General Abdul Rahim Wardak had been the MinDef since 2004, a professional soldier and Mujahidin Leader from the majority Pashtun Tribes - around half a population of around 31 million. Well respected by his own people, with his excellent spoken and written English, he was a Statesman whom most of the International Community liked dealing with. Four months I worked for him, until he resigned after being impeached by Afghan Parliamentarians after rocket attacks over the border from Pakistan went unchallenged - as they had been for 40 years.

He was often a hard task master, very shrewd and knowledgeable, but I soon gained his trust, especially on developing diplomatic opportunities for him. He was well known by the senior military leaders in theatre and in the Defence Ministries of many nations but my job was to improve his relationships with the Civilian Politicians and Diplomats through the Office of the NATO Special Representative to Afghanistan, working with the ISAF Commander who had overall responsibility for all military aspects of the operation.

I continued this from September 2012 for the new MinDef, Besmellah Kahn Mohammadi (Min BKM) a Tajik -around 27% of population - and a self-schooled soldier from the Panjshir Valley who had been a senior military leader under 'the Great Massoud' during the war against the Communists, Soviets, Al Qaeda and the Taliban.

He was a previous Chief of the General Staff under General Wardak. His focus was solely on developing the ANA to take over from ISAF, defeat the Taliban and other insurgents and then perhaps retire back to the Panjshir Valley. I operated with UK MOD's blessing but not much else, and was pretty independent, usually turning up at the BEK for a couple of hours to work with the Political and Defence Staffs until the Consular Building was made secure for the night. I had to sort out answers to the matters concerning UK MOD, Foreign Office or other Government Departments (OGDs) needed for the Afghan MOD Leaders, the next day. These ranged from forthcoming diplomatic visits, information requests and working through Memorandums of Understanding for specific UK / Afghan requirements. Not many dull days! All the Senior

CAPTIONS: Nick receiving a leaving gift from Besmellah Khan Mohammadi (Afghan Minister of Defence)

Leadership of the Afghan MOD, with the exception of the First Deputy Minister, held military rank and had significant personal experience fighting the enemies of Afghanistan. Their Personal Security Teams or trusted Afghan Bodyguards were mainly war veterans as well, which was a little unnerving but very interesting for a civilian.

In Afghanistan Relationships are Everything

My relationship with the MinDef and his team developed, as did their level of trust and confidence in me to press home the benefits of increasing and improving political and diplomatic engagements with the international community.

I needed to develop strong relationships with all the Afghans I worked with, partly to get the job done but also to increase my chances of survival. Nothing was known about the backgrounds of the soldiers who guarded the leadership, many spoke little or no English and they were very well armed. Insider Threat - or Green-on-Blue - Attacks were not rare and to date 143 coalition troops have been killed and 181 wounded since 2008. The Minister and other senior leaders consider these attacks cowardly, disrespectful and without honour and I was asked to draft a number of letters of condolence to the Defence Ministers of many of the Coalition Nations who had lost men and women as a result of these attacks.

Travelling around Afghanistan with the MinDef was exciting in military fixed and rotary wing flights to places like Kandahar, Helmand, Herat and the Panjshir Valley. Sometimes our greeting was gunfire from the insurgency. I also supported the Minister on a number of Defence Ministerial Visits to NATO HQ in Brussels.

A particularly memorable event was Min BKM's 'Guest of Government' visit to the UK in February 2013. This entailed high profile visits to the MOD and Foreign Office for discussions with Senior Political and Military Leaders, including both Secretaries of State, and a day at RMC Sandhurst with Afghan Cadets followed by a trip to Windsor to meet

The Afghan Delegation in Brussels (Nick 2nd left)

the Coldstream Guards readying themselves for a deployment to Afghanistan. A second 'notable occasion' was the opening of the ANA Officer Academy with our own SofS and President Hamid Karzai in attendance. Trying to coordinate the Afghan and UK MOD interface was a challenge and it was an immensely proud moment watching it all work so well on the day. Sadly the President's Security was so strict that no cameras or phones were allowed – his Personal Security Team was most thorough and it took 15 minutes to make it through all the searches.

What Happened Next – After Action Review

Working long days for nearly two years in a Ministerial Office in Kabul was a challenge. No amount of training prepared me for protecting myself every day and, whilst I was under close protection much of the time, I had to trust the Afghans that I worked with in this dangerous environment. I have witnessed death and destruction by IEDs and Suicide Bombers, but felt lucky to come home to the normality of life in the UK. The last 13 years of the International Community's military and civil involvement has not been wasted and I believe that the MOD and the ANA will continue to improve security so that democracy will flourish.

Afghanistan is a truly mesmerising place with its rich culture. If any nation and its population deserve peace in our time then the Afghans must be very close to the top of that sadly very long list and HG Wells Poignant Quotation is so true here.

Nick received the OBE in the Queen's Birthday Honours. The official citation reads:"Nicholas John Carter – Defence Advisor – Ministry of Defence. For services to Defence Restructuring in Afghanistan."

DIABETES – *dangerous and deadly!*

"DIABETES is the only major disease with a death rate that is still rising . . . so far there is no cure." "Two thirds of people with Diabetes will develop heart disease."

"Nearly 80% of diabetics die of heart disease or stroke."

"Diabetes consumes over 10% of the cost of health care and diabetics account for over 15% of hospital admissions."

All these attention grabbing headlines indicate the seriousness of the disease . . . but

What is DIABETES ?

HERE Dr. Andrew Macklin, a Consultant Diabetologist at Dorset County Hospital, and member of the Editorial Board of the British Journal of Diabetes and Vascular Disease, gives an expert's 'take' on the subject.

Diabetes – an overview by Dr. Andrew Macklin

DIABETES mellitus is a common disease, described in medical texts stretching back into ancient history. The "Diabetes" part of the name arises from the observation that the sufferer passes large volumes of urine due to the high blood glucose level. The "Mellitus" part relates to the limited laboratory testing available in the distant past and distinguishes Diabetes Mellitus, when the urine tastes like honey, from Diabetes Insipidus, where it tastes like water.

We all have some glucose in our blood and need to keep it that way in order to keep organs such as our brain functioning and to transport carbohydrate around the body so that it can be stored within the muscles for instant access when bursts of activity/ power are required. In diabetes the control systems that keep the blood glucose levels stable become weakened, broken or overwhelmed and the blood glucose levels rise.

How do we decide how high a blood glucose has to be before it is too high? In order to answer this we actually need to discuss the consequences of diabetes (we will assume the "Mellitus" part from here on).

Short Term Effects and Complications

As mentioned already, there are short term effects from having high blood glucose levels. These are sometimes the reason for a patient seeking the help of their doctor.

They include thirst, passing large volumes of urine during the day and having to get up frequently to pass urine at night. Fatigue or infections such as thrush or boils may be more prominent in some people. These symptoms are the direct effect of the high glucose levels and resolve with treatment. While they can get dramatically out of control and result in hospital admissions these symptoms are usually picked up and treated fairly easily now that we have access to simpler, more accurate and less disgusting testing equipment.

Other effects of diabetes also occur, more insidiously, and these are typically referred to as diabetes complications. These are due to damage to the tiniest blood vessels in the body. For reasons that are only partly understood there is a level of

Diabetes UK advert

glucose which the body requires, a range above that which it can cope with and a higher level at which there is damage to small blood vessels throughout the body. These tiny vessels, called capillaries, develop weakened walls and can either stretch excessively or become blocked. As a consequence the normal delivery of blood to the tissues is disturbed, with leakage of fluid through the capillary walls or lack of blood to the tissues leading to damage and loss of function.

The typical body areas to show signs of this damage are the retina in the eye, the nerves especially in the feet and legs and the kidney. These areas are the subject of regular screening and testing once a person has been diagnosed with diabetes.

Blood sugar levels, insulin and glucose control

We can define diabetes as the blood sugar level which is high enough to cause damage and for this purpose it is easiest to use the retinal changes, since these are easiest to measure and they have a characteristic appearance when they arise from diabetes. Careful testing and analysis of the relationship of blood glucose to the development of complications has allowed us to use simple tests such as fasting blood sugar levels and HbA1c (a measure of the glucose that gets "stuck" to the red cells over time) to make the diagnosis as well as to measure the current level of control.

It may already have occurred to you that while we have a disease (damage to small blood vessels), with an identified cause for the damage (high blood sugar) that this cannot be the whole of the story as there must be something abnormal to cause the high blood sugar levels. In other words, for diabetes to actually develop there must be a problem with the glucose control systems.

Blood sugar level is reduced by insulin (a hormone produced in the pancreas), starvation and exercise. It is increased by eating carbohydrates (which your body digests into glucose). There are other hormones which affect glucose levels but we'll try and keep things fairly simple. Insulin is secreted into the blood stream, attaches to receptors on the surface of cells and causes glucose to be taken out of the blood and turned into either quick access energy stores (glycogen) or fat. It also decreases the production of new glucose from the liver – it is the release of stored glucose that keeps the blood sugars stable overnight, when you are not eating.

If there is not enough insulin production then the cells in the body are not told to take up enough glucose from the blood and the blood glucose level rises. Alternatively, if the cells do not respond well enough to the insulin signal then they need higher levels to get the same effect (insulin resistance). Once the requirements for insulin are high enough they exceed the ability of the pancreas to make enough insulin and the blood glucose level rises.

There are many causes of rising insulin resistance, often with several contributing to the problem in the same person. Lack of exercise, obesity and aging are the most common. It is this combination which is responsible for the explosion of diabetes in the western world, with some states in the USA having 1 in 5 adults diagnosed.

You will probably have heard of type 2 diabetes, which in most cases is due to this insulin resistant state. You may also have come across people who clearly are not old, overweight, immobile or in any fashion likely to have type 2 diabetes. These are often children or young adults who develop diabetes symptoms very rapidly and not infrequently need a hospital admission to stabilise their metabolism with insulin. These people have type 1 diabetes, which is caused by lack of insulin production. In type 1 diabetes the body develops an immune response to the insulin producing cells of its own pancreas and destroys them, leaving nothing to produce insulin with. The lack of insulin leads to rocketing blood glucose levels and the production of chemicals called ketones, which are acidic and upset the body pH balance in a potentially fatal fashion. It is this dramatic and life threatening presentation, together with the age and challenges of replacing insulin levels with injections that has lead to a common misconception that type 1 diabetes is serious and type 2 diabetes is more trivial.

Increasing complications

Diabetes complications arise in proportion to the average amount of excess glucose in the blood, the duration of the diabetes and factors that affect blood vessel health, such as smoking and high blood pressure. Someone with newly diagnosed type 1 diabetes will have only had high glucose levels for a short time before the diagnosis is made. Someone with type 2 diabetes may well have the diagnosis made 5 years or so after the glucose levels first became damaging, such is the insidious nature of its onset. In the days when "geriatrics" were those people who were past retirement age there was less lifetime for people with type 2 diabetes to get the specific diabetes complications. Also, early deaths from heart attacks and strokes would have been hard to detect in those less health conscious days. Nowadays diabetes care and general health care are good enough that we see the majority of advanced diabetes complications in people with type 2 diabetes. Worryingly this is likely to increase as the more sedentary lifestyle and weight problems currently seen in the US tend to predict the state of the UK in 10-20 years.

It should be mentioned that there is a very long list of causes of diabetes that are neither type 1 nor type 2. It is the job of the health professional making the diagnosis to consider these possible causes and to arrange the necessary tests/reviews. I will omit a whole textbook's worth of discussion here about genetics, hormones, minerals, surgeons, drugs and pregnancy.

Prevention

Prevention is better than treatment and there is good evidence that losing weight and exercising have benefits in many aspects of health, including the development of diabetes. People at high risk of diabetes who joined a US trial of diet and exercise were able to reduce their chance of progressing to diabetes by 2/3 by losing 7% of their body weight and taking 150 minutes of moderate intensity exercise per week (i.e. half an hour 5 days per week, not much more than a brisk walk to work and back).

INDEPENDENT DIABETES TRUST

Understanding Your Diabetes

HELPLINE: 01604 622837
www.iddtinternational.org

Booklet by the Independent Diabetes Trust

Even if diabetes cannot be prevented there are treatments that can reduce the chance of developing complications. Major trials in both type 1 and type 2 diabetes have shown that the risk of developing complications in the eyes, feet and kidneys can be reduced by 60% by careful control of the glucose to near normal levels. This tight control is not without its problems and when drugs such as insulin or certain of the oral treatments are used there is a risk of dropping the blood sugar too low and causing a "hypo". Hypos are usually relatively minor, from a health professional point of view, and cause sweating, trembling, hunger and an unpleasant feeling of malaise. They can, if untreated and if seriously low blood glucose levels develop, proceed to mental confusion and stupefaction and even to fits.

Trials have been carried out to determine whether entirely normal glucose levels are a desirable target once diabetes has been diagnosed. These have shown that once the diabetes requires medication that can cause low glucose levels the target level of blood sugar needs to be a little higher, so as to give a larger safety margin. For diet treatment, tablets that don't cause hypos and for one specific type of injectable treatment there is less reason not to aim for blood glucose levels as normal as possible.

We screen (i.e. test before the patient has symptoms) for the development of diabetes complications, as well as the risk factors for developing complications, such as blood pressure. This is usually done on an annual basis and if early problems are identified this allows the use of treatments that reduce the risk of this early damage progressing. As a result of early identification and effective treatment of diabetes complications the health of people diagnosed with diabetes is improving. Even if complications do progress the rate is slowed and treatment for the more advanced stages can be discussed and planned with the patient.

In the early 20th century type 1 diabetes was often a death sentence with a life expectancy worse than many cancers. By the middle of the 20th century deaths from untreated type 1 diabetes were hugely outnumbered by the deaths due to complications such as kidney disease. By the end of the last century the data from Finland suggested that only about 7% of people with type 1 diabetes were developing aggressive diabetes kidney disease. There is still a lot of work to do to cure type 1 diabetes and to help people with the other sorts of diabetes live healthy and enjoyable lives.

Those of us with diabetes and those people who hope to avoid it in later life need to try and be as slim, fit & healthy as we can manage – even if you can't avoid diabetes forever the later you get the high blood glucose levels the less time they have to do you harm.

DRUMMER HODGE

The much talked about, thought provoking, musical community play by Rupert Creed, based on a short poem of the same name by Thomas Hardy, inspired this work by regular poetry contributor Devina Symes

Looking through our County's history books

informs us of past triumphs and trials

yet scanning the old photographs within

we can't imagine what's behind the smiles.

That is until through the community play

forgotten stories, generations have ignored

take on a new life through the writer's pen

and the dead souls rise, fully restored.

Drummer Hodge is a poignant poem

penned by Thomas Hardy, in memory

of all the 'Hodges' who served their county

marching to foreign lands, willingly.

And it was this Hardy poem that inspired

Dorchester's latest community play,

where the audience is transported back in time

to witness Hodge's life, day by day.

With drums banging and cymbals clanging,

the stage is set, the atmosphere, alive.

As mists eerily swirl and images unfurl,

emotionally, we wonder- how will he survive?

From a distance it's easy to think cosy

and wallow in the victories of war

much harder to face harsh reality

to ask yourself, "what was it all for?"

Yet this is what happened in Dorchester

where rich and poor split their loyalties

and only through love and forgiveness

was peace restored to those families.

The circle of life is encompassed in this play

and to all those past souls we owe a huge debt

they taught us that grief can be
transmuted by a belief

in each other: let's honour them,
and never forget.

Devina Symes

Thomas Hardy recalled that all agriculture workers who served their county were known as 'Hodge'
His young protagonist was killed in the Boer War.

A CHILD'S VIEW OF LIFE IN THE BARRACKS AT DORCHESTER 1925 – 1935

by Bob Manning

MY father was Victor Manning who served in the Dorset Regiment from 1911 to 1936 including a spell at the Barracks at Dorchester from 1923 until his retirement in 1936.

It is nearly 80 years since my father retired from the Army and we left the Barracks. I was about 10 years old when we left.

For those unfamiliar with military terminology The Depot Barracks was the barracks where new recruits came for basic training, before being posted to one of the two battalions. The Permanent Staff at the Depot were the trained soldiers who taught the recruits. At the Marabout Barracks the Permanent Staff were soldiers, normally Warrant Officers or NCOs, responsible for training the part time soldiers of the Territorial Army.

There were quite a lot of children resident in the two Barracks during those years so we were never short of someone to play with. We organised our own entertainment and amusement and could always find something to do.

Within certain limits we were pretty free to roam about and were not troubled by too many rules and regulations, provided we used common sense. The Permanent

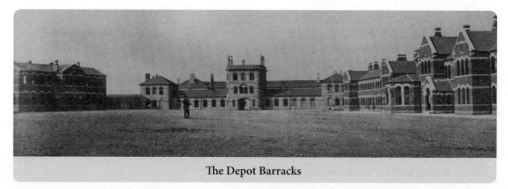

The Depot Barracks

Staff were normally friendly. Many of them were fathers so, looking back from a parent's point of view, we were pretty safe.

The Depot Barracks were behind The Keep and the site on the other side of Poundbury Road was the Marabout Barracks, the home of the Territorial Army.

As children we were not allowed to enter the Depot Barracks through The Keep on our own. We had to go round by Poundbury Road and up "The Steps" which provided a pedestrian access between the two Barracks.   There was very little traffic in the Poundbury Road in those days. None of the Industrial Estates existed, nor the housing estates further up the road. The junction with St Thomas Road by the railway bridge marked the end of the town and, apart from Whitfield Farm, there was nothing until Bradford Peverell.

On either side of the Keep entrance were two great guns from the First World War. These were removed for scrap metal during the Second World War. I can remember father taking us into the Keep and taking us out on to the balcony on the front as well as up onto the roof.

The Keep - Depot Barracks

Next in from The Keep, the soldiers' quarters were very strictly "out of bounds" to we children, though I can remember being taken on a tour of these by my father and RSM Hodge.

Part of the next building was a NAAFI store. We were often sent there by Mother to get groceries, but I expect that soldiers would have used this for cigarettes, dubbin, brasso and the inevitable blanco.The other part of the building was the Sergeants' Mess and beyond that was a house that we occupied from about 1933 until my father retired.

I remember the bank between us and the railway was grass covered with an iron railing at the top. During the spring of each year the grass on the bank was allowed to grow quite long until it was cut by scythe. This was then used by the boys from the Married Quarters for making "forts". It was then that I first heard the word "sangar" from some of the old North West Frontier soldiers. Our "sangars" though were made of grass rather than stone

I recall that we could get some of the "old soldiers" to talk of their experiences in India but they would not talk about the Great War, even the men from the 2nd Battalion, like my father, who had spent the War in Mesopotamia and Palestine rather than on the Western Front.

The Married Quarters were in a two storied building consisting of four or five "quarters" on each level with an iron staircase at each end and a walkway along the front on the upper storey. Playing "chase" up one stairway, along the walkway and down the other staircase was strictly forbidden – not that is to say that the prohibition was always heeded. It was too good a chance for boys to miss!

Behind the married quarters was the Schoolroom. This was for soldiers –not children. In front was a grassy area that girls used for skipping and ball games. At times there were soldier exams and we children were kept away.

To the north of the site were stables for the officers' horses. If there were no officers about we would go and look at the horses. The stalls backed on to a grassy area and fronted a cobbled area with a low wall and a high metal railing.

We could look through the railing at the horses and chat to the soldiers doing grooming and cleaning the stable area. This was only of passing interest though and not one of our normal routines.

The Square we were very definitely NOT allowed to walk on. At the end, nearest The Keep, was a small round white painted circle. At certain times of the day a bugler would come out of the Guardroom in The Keep, march smartly up to the circle and blow the appropriate call. He would then march smartly back and things would happen! Usually this only entailed the recruits pouring out of the barrack rooms on to the Square and forming up, or going to the gym or something similar. As boys we got to know the meanings of many of the calls but it did not affect us very much. Later, during the war, I found I could still recall many of the bugle calls. Not now though, too long ago!

In front of the Officers Mess was a small grass area where bivouac tents would be erected, and on other places around both barrack sites, for a week or two when visiting regiments came for an exercise or other activity. We would try to get cap or other badges but were not usually successful! They were not so easily available as in the war years.

The Marabout Barracks

That was the "Depot" as we called it.

At some stage we moved down to the Married Quarters in the Marabout Barracks, possibly for bigger accommodation as we were a growing family. We would spend Saturday afternoons watching football and hockey on the sports field close by.

One of our joys as boys when we lived in the Married Quarters was to watch the T.A. Band practising marching and countermarching. Opposite were workshops run by civilian staff. We were not supposed to "hang around" those workshops but small boys could "dilly-dally" when walking past, hoping for an invitation to see what was going on. Couldn't they?

There was a Medical Centre with Colonel Sidgwick in charge. As children we, of course, knew Col. Sidgwick who treated our childish ailments; measles and flu, and gave us inoculations and so on. He was a tall lean chap, or at least seemed so to small children, with a sort of "hospital aroma" about him.

There were pigsties kept by a soldier called Frampton. At least we thought he was a soldier but looking back he may have been a civilian employee. A group of us, with nothing better to do, would go down and look at the pigs and talk to Mr Frampton. Again looking back I seem to recall that we always spoke of him, and to him, as Mr Frampton. Memory is a curious thing.

The Depot C.O, Major De la Bere, lived in a house outside the perimeter wall but there was a door through which he would come on his way to the Depot. If we were wearing caps we were expected to raise them to him if he passed us. He always acknowledged such action and sometimes would speak to us asking what game we were playing and how we were getting on. The usual "adult to small children" approach!

There were a number of trees around and this was our "woodland" – to small boys an area to play Robin Hood or Red Indians or the current "comic" heroes from "The Wizard" or "The Hotspur". Trying to look back there were probably no more than 15-18 trees but again to small boys it seemed more. I wonder if any of those trees still exist?

Apart from the grass "sangars" I do not recall that we played much in the way of "soldier" or army games. Whether we were not encouraged to do so because the memory of the Great War was still upon the country and therefore impinged on our childish minds I do not now know. Remember that the older boys aged 15 or16 in the late 1920s would have grown up in a wartime atmosphere and would have seen the dreaded "Deeply Regret" telegrams arrive.

It is difficult at this distance of time to remember and distinguish between the Great War affect upon childish minds with those of my teenage memories of the gathering war clouds in the late 1930s. Certainly we were aware, children though we were, of the Great War's continuing impact upon people's minds.

For diversion there was Poundbury. This was long before the present day industrial site was built. It was then all just green grass until the war expanded the barracks. There was some sort of gateway, down by the pigsties, which got us onto the slopes of the hill fort and then up over the rampart and the railway tunnel entrance and so into the interior. I think at one time or another most of us would climb through the fence onto the railway line and "bravely" set foot in the tunnel for just a few yards. There were boys who claimed to have walked right through the tunnel.

On weekend days and in the holidays we would 'picnic' either as a gang or with family. Along the Poundbury road by the hill fort, and for some way on, was a rather scrubby line of trees and bushes which we called Sherwood Forest and in which we played various games. We would also get on the lower slopes and work our way round to the river. Many lads would swim and bathe there or just paddle about.

There was not a lot of association between the barracks' children and those outside. Even though at the time there was quite a lot of family housing in The Grove, Bridport Road, St Thomas Road and Cornwall Road we in the barracks tended to keep to ourselves.

Many of us in the 8-10 age range belonged to the Misses Hannay's Cub Scout Pack - the "1st Dorchester Wolf Cub Pack" - which met in a hut in the grounds of their house in what is now Hawthorne Road; the house and hut are long since demolished. Their father was General Hannay but we went there because it was close to the Barracks and not because of a military connection. My sister - born 1927 - remembers going to Brownies at the Medical Centre.

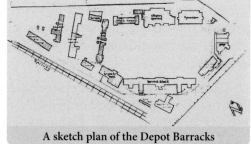

I do not recall any officially organised Christmas parties for the barracks children or anything in the way of games or sports or other entertainments.

My younger brother Gordon – born 1929 - has a recollection as a small boy

A sketch plan of the Depot Barracks

of riding a child's "motor car" down the hill from the Poundbury Road and crashing into the pigsties at the bottom, making a hole in the wall. There would not have been a lot of vehicular traffic along that road, just cycle riding and primitive go-carting down the hill.

The road would have been one of our "play areas" with the sloping bank continuing round the bottom of the football field and along the wall to the back of the TA Drill Hall.

So there it was, a happy time with plenty of friends and things to do.

It did not give me a taste for Army life – even though I was conscripted during WWII.

From the Year Book – 100 Years Ago

Society historian and archivist the Rev. Dr. John C. Travell FRSA reports

ITEMS from the Year Book for 1915-1916

FROM the beginning, the Year Books have included articles from or about people who had first-hand memories of life in Dorset stretching back through the previous century. Among these was the Society's first President, Sir Frederick Treves, who was a regular contributor.

William Barnes

Treves was born in Cornhill, Dorchester in 1853, and provided an article on 'William Barnes' the Dorset Poet' whose school in South Street he attended. He describes South Street in the 1860s as 'a causeway through a world-forgotten town that a writer of a century ago described as "the most antique looking little town that she had ever seen." . . . It was a street of private houses of a respectability so pronounced and a contentment so complete as to be almost oppressive.'

South Street then was very different from the main shopping street it has now become, although looking up above the shop fronts which have replaced the private gardens, you can still see some of the big houses which once lined the street. The only shop in the street in those days was a shoe-makers . . .'There was one house behind high gates that had a carriage drive.' Another house had a front garden with lawns and peacocks. Treves said that 'on an old map of. . .1771, this garden is shown as part of the extensive pleasure grounds owned by Mr. William Templeman'. Farm carts used to trundle down the street to 'the great cornfields' that 'came down in a vast sweep' at the end of South Street to Beggar's Knap.

Treves goes on to describe "The picturesque Figure of Barnes", detailing his curious clothes and his indifference to his appearance. Barnes, he says, was self-educated, and he gives an impressive account of his skills and achievements as a philologist, mathematician, and as an authority on social science and political economy. He was an antiquarian, a skilled wood-engraver, who illustrated many of his own books and carved his own chessmen. He played the organ, piano, violin and flute, and spoke Latin, Greek, French, German, Italian, Spanish, Hindustani, Persian, Arabic and Welsh. He produced a commercial dictionary and published an Anglo-Saxon delectus and invented swimming shoes. He had over 90 published works. Speaking of the Dorset dialect as ' a pure and ancient language' Treves quotes Barnes as saying that it was a remnant of the speech of King Alfred, and that "if the Court had not moved to London . . .(it) would have been the Court language of today."

Treves describes becoming a pupil in Barnes's school in 1860 when he was seven years old. "The schoolroom was a temporary structure of two storeys, built at the back of the house in what would have been the garden. The pupils entered by means of an outside wooden stair, accessible from what was then called Back South Street. The first lesson he received from Barnes was a lecture on logic, which he found 'wholly unintelligible.' Barnes, he says, was popular with the boys, extremely absent-minded, and treated them kindly, being very unlike the harsh Victorian schoolmasters described by Dickens.

Swanage in the 19th century

The Society's immediate past President, Sir Stephen Collins, submitted an article on "The Swanage of My Boyhood", looking back sixty years to before the railways came, saying, "My earliest teens were at the time of the Crimean War." He recalled that many of his contemporaries worked in the stone quarries from seven years of age. The only education was from Sunday Schools run by the churches. 'A Superintendent of the Congregational School, who adorned that office for over fifty years', gave elocution lessons on Sunday afternoons. Collins' father was a quarry owner, and only the sons of the quarrymen were given apprenticeships. The Purbeck stone was stacked along the shore and transported by ship to London and other towns and cities where it was used in the building of town halls, churches, hotels and theatres in the great nineteenth century building boom.

The Great War

Inevitably, the progress of the war was a predominant theme for the Year Book in 1915, with reports on the fields of action of the Dorset Regiment. Photos of 'Ten sons and a son-in-law of Alfred Pope serving in the forces of 1915' show how deeply the war was involving Dorset families. A lecture on 'The Dorset Regiment in War' was given to the Society by Field-Marshall Sir Evelyn Wood VC , which included accounts of the Monmouth rebellion of 1685, and the Regiment's fight in 1845, under Sir Charles Napier, with Baluchi robbers in the Trakhi Hills in India, during which a 'sergeant's party of 15 men of the 39th ' climbed up a mountain crater where 2000

Baluchi were besieged. They were all killed in hand-to-hand fighting, but even the Baluchi were impressed by and acknowledged their foolhardy bravery. Wood went on to give a detailed account of two battles on 1 May and 13 October, 1915, when 'a battalion of the Regiment continued to fight determinedly . . . even after a loss of fifty per centum.'

Harry Pouncy also gave one of his annual lectures to the Society on 'The Great War and Dorset's share in it' at a meeting chaired by Colonel (later Lieutenant-General) Louis Bols DSO, who had taken the Dorsets into war in 1914. He had been wounded and captured by the Germans at Givenchy in November 1914 but had managed to escape and return to his regiment.

Princess Catherine Radziwill

The Society had received two letters addressed from Princess Catherine Radziwill, described as 'a member of the Russian royal family', headed 'My call to Dorset'. In the first of these she writes about 'how the war came to Russia' and 'how the poor people . . . heard the voice of their beloved Tsar calling upon them to rise up and help him.' She appeals to Dorset 'Do your best, so long as there are young men in your land, and go and meet the enemy who is menacing you . . . I call upon you Dorset men to rise, and to pour more of your fine regiments into the fields of conflict in the name of the poor Russian peasants who have given all they had. . .' Her second letter, dated 29 October 1915, was addressed directly to the Editor of the Dorset Year Book, Newman Flower, and is a further appeal to the men of Dorset following the execution of nurse Edith Cavell by a German firing squad in Belgium on 12 October 1915. Her death resulted in a great deal of anger against the Germans who were condemned as brutal murderers. In her letter Princess Radziwill wrote, 'Tell this to your Dorset men. . . and bid them never to forget Edith Cavell, nor her martyrdom which she endured for a cause which I feel sure they will be more eager now to defend than they ever were before.'

Newman Flower also wrote about 'What the Dorsets have done in the Great War' giving accounts of the engagements in which the Dorsets were involved ' as far as could be known at the time.' The First Battalion went to Flanders as part of the original Expeditionary Force, while the Second Battalion were sent to the Persian Gulf. The Territorials were in India with the Dorset Battery of Artillery, and the Fifth Dorsets in the Dardanelles: 'the Dorset Yeomanry was grievously cut up in the spring of this year in Gallipoli . . .in forty-eight hours three-quarters of the strength of a Dorset regiment fell in defending a patch of conquered soil.' On May 1, and again on 5 and 6, on Hill 60 in France, the Dorsets were the first to be attacked by the Germans with gas; but the wind then changed direction and gassed the German trenches as well.

The Society's response to the War

In an article 'Round the Year with the Dorset Men' , William Watkins reported on the Society's response to the war: providing comforts for 'our County Regiments', the ladies knitting gloves, socks and mittens. Money gifts had come from India, China, Africa, Australia, New Zealand, the Solomon Islands and many other remote corners of the empire, and also from friends in America.

At the Society's AGM, Watkins was congratulated for having his name included in the Commission of the Peace of the County of Dorset. It was also reported that the Comfort Fund had made generous gifts of money, tobacco, cigarettes, brandy balls, Christmas puddings, football shirts, cricket things, bugles, mouth organs, and games which had been sent to France and other places where the Dorsets were serving. Watkins had received a letter from Lt. Col. John Bateman of the 1 Battalion, the Dorset Regiment, writing from the trenches, thanking him for the gifts. A concert was given by Miss Susie Boyle and her pupils at the Hampstead Conservatoire in aid of the Fund. The programme for this included a poem by Stanley Galpin which said: 'Let those who can go forth to fight, and may God speed them on their way; For those too old it is but right that they should stop at home – and pay.'

News from Australia

The Dorset Men in Sydney, in the report from their AGM in 1915, had received a letter from one of their members who was the captain of a minesweeper. He gave an account of the landing of troops in the Dardanelles:'As we landed them in boats the Turks smothered them with shrapnel . . . then our poor beggars had to jump out, wade ashore through barbed wire entanglements laid in the sea, and storm high cliffs where the Turks were strongly entrenched on top . . . they were just lying on the beach by the hundreds, poor beggars, as if they were asleep.'

The contributions from Australia also included accounts of two people who had migrated there from Dorset during the 19th Century. Samuel George, who was born in Blandford in 1827, had joined the gold rush to California in 1850. He described the hardships endured by the prospectors as they sought their fortunes. On one occasion he was so hard up that he sold his boots for an ounce of gold. He succeeded in staking a claim and began to employ other men. One of these had been an overseer of slaves and described stripping and thrashing girl slaves. In 1854 he went to Australia to join the gold rush there, where he found that conditions were very much tougher than they had been in California.

The death in Sydney was reported of Mrs. Joseph Notting who had been born in Poole in 1817. Her grandfather was George Kemp whose large house 'The Fish Ponds, Poole, had become the Cornelia Hospital. Mrs. Notting and her husband had left for Australia in 1854, a voyage which had taken 120 days. 'Up to a few days of her decease

The Old Cornelia Hospital

. . . she could relate the starting of the railway in England and in New South Wales, the old method of open voting at elections, the passing of the Reform Bill, the window tax, the corn laws and anti-slavery agitation.' When she landed in Sydney rents were abnormally dear through the gold rush. Dr. J. D. Jones of Bournemouth (the famous Congregationalist preacher of Richmond Hill) visited her on 2 August 1914. 'She was enthusiastic about the late Mr. Henniker Heaton's scheme for the penny postage throughout the world. She remembered that it had cost ninepence to send a letter from Poole to London.'

"Hat's the way to do it!"
- a resounding local success

The Bridport Hat Festival by Roger Snook

WHEN John F Kennedy described the hat as a useless appendage the hat industry was, at that time the early 60s - in decline. His statement sounded the death knell and the hatting industries virtually disappeared, except for millinery creations and a few stalwarts such as the bowler and top hats. The British Hat Council tried to beat the decline with clever slogans such as, 'If you want to get ahead wear a hat'. Regrettably their efforts were to no avail.

I had to wear a straw boater for most of my schooling in Swaziland: this was regarded as a last vestige of the Empire but the custom taught one the etiquette of wearing of a hat, since when my interest in men's headwear has never waned and now my little emporium - T Snook at 32 West Street, Bridport - started by my grandfather as a gentlemen's outfitters - is one of the most comprehensive hat shops in England.

An exciting new event

Fifty years after those colonial schooldays I found myself starting up The Bridport Hat Festival, the first such event of its kind in the UK. News of the Festival spread throughout the UK hat industry, which adopted it with enthusiasm. It turned out we were all waiting for something very like it to happen, it just needed a destination, an untapped enthusiasm from someone 'in the know' and a population willing to run with an exciting new event.

What I had not realised at the time was that Bridport, with its legacy of rope and net-making, had also been a centre of the straw, hemp and flax-weaving and hat-making industry back in the18th century, when the French revolution prohibited imports from France reaching our shores. The industry was short-lived but in its day

Hats Off

employed great numbers of young girls and women, giving them a craft-based skill and a working wage.

The Hat Festival is held in mid September each year and is an event at which people can lose all inhibitions about wearing hats, sporting their fun, fancy, quirky, retro, stylish, perched and home-made concoctions. People dig out family heirlooms, occasion hats only worn once, even uniform headwear: it brings out the humour and whimsy in everyone and is a place where one's true character really emerges.

As well as the fun element there is the more serious side. The 'Milliners and Hatters Open Competition' attracts milliners from around the world, with prize money amounting to £900 and entries coming from as far-a-field as Australia, America and Canada for the best millinery creation. Entries are produced to the highest standard of workmanship. Last year saw the first Dorset millinery creation take the £500 top prize.

The highlight of the Festival is at lunchtime on Saturday, when a mass photoshoot, photographed from on high, takes place in Bucky Doo Square. With thousands of people bedecked in headwear of every description this is quite a spectacle to behold. The mass photoshoot is followed by judging and prize-giving for best ladies', gents', boys' and girls' hats, and the most elegantly-hatted couple. It's a must for audience participation.

The Bridport Hat Festival has been described as one of Dorset's quickest festivals, with attendance growing in just five years to an estimated 10,000. With the continued support of the community this is one event that can only get bigger and better.

Roger Snook

Brewery Horses

By Kay Ennals MBE

Early morn in the brewery yard,
noisy beer barrels rolling . . .
Hops and malt pervaded the air
. . . A busy day was starting.

Strong arms lifted heavy casks,
men worked too on other tasks.
More barrels were rolled up from the
store, until the dray could take no more.

Draught horses in their stables waited impatiently,
They were ready to work at this early hour, their willing muscles gleamed with power.
"We'll need two", the carter decided, "bring out our handsome white shires".
Drummer and Joey tossed their heads. They were chosen for strength, like their sires.

Horse-shoes clanged as metal struck stone and the Shires walked up through the
town to the yard, to be hitched to the heavy dray
. . . harnessed to haul throughout the day!

"Walk on, walk on" the two were told.
They heaved and pulled at the laden load.
Gradually wheels began to turn, then Drummer and Joey pounded the road.

In Weymouth and Portland barrels were left . . . the dray was now much lighter.
The horses had to rest the night . . . just empties to take back tomorrow. . .
to the brewery yard!

The sculpture of "Drummer" stands in Brewery Square, Dorchester, as a tribute to the last dray horses that worked at the Eldridge Pope site in the 1970s.

Artist Shirley Pace, 81, came out of retirement to complete the project.

The Parachute Regiment Padre

by Allan Cooper

FATHER Bernard EGAN SJ asked me "What was your former occupation?" "I was a schoolmaster," I said.

Father Egan went on to say that he was Chaplain at St. Mary's School, Shaftesbury, and asked if I would like to visit.

I rode my motorcycle down the ZigZag Hill north of Sixpenny Handley. I took a camera.

Before looking round we had coffee. Behind Father Egan's desk was a large painting by David Shepherd of The Bridge Too Far. "That painting was given me by the Parachute Regiment."

Father Egan at St. Mary's School, Shaftesbury

He went on to say that he dropped into the Battle at Arnhem carrying the elements of Holy Communion. Wounded and dying paratroopers were lying together in a damaged house. While tending their needs Father Egan was shot in the leg. The order was given to retreat and leave soldiers who were unable to walk.

Father Egan by the leaning tree

Before I left St. Mary's School we walked on park land. I noticed a leaning evergreen tree and asked "Why isn't that tree upright?" Father Egan said, "It's a variety called Wellingtonia Inclinate." I believed him and wrote to Kew Gardens. "Someone is pulling your leg."

I 'phoned Father Egan and we had a good laugh. He went on to say "The tree was damaged in a storm." He added "By the way, I am going to retire from St. Mary's School and live in the Jesuit retirement house of St. Bueno in North Wales. It could be called the Jesuit knacker's yard."

**Allan Cooper at home in
Wimborne St. Giles.**

Allan T. P. Cooper BA FRSA has been a valued contributor to the Dorset Year Book for over half a century, never having become a member of The Society of Dorset Men.

The Committee, in acknowledgment of his support over so many years, has awarded him Life Membership of the Society.

His first piece – a poem from the 1958/59 edition – is published below.

A DORSET WIND

From the wild sea it sprang

clawing at the hurrying clouds:

but, frustrated by their flight,

directed its terror earthwards

driving up and over the Downs

flattening, in a trice,

a million grass-blades

into a nodding obeisance.

And so Nature, in Her wisdom,

yielded but did not succumb.

Not so with the Husbandman.

His stately delicate beauties,

possessed of seeming bounteous grace,

they would not bend to

the transitory day-long storm.

They, which were contrived by Man

to perfect the work of providence,

fell irreparably to lie

all summer long a grim reminder

that, although held more fair,

Husbandry is as naught

in the trial of the wind.

God's grass springeth up as new:

Man's staple,

lying too heavy

in the head to stand again,

need be gathered up

as best it may.

Allan T. P. Cooper

PALMERS BREWERY- A 221 YEAR SUCCESS STORY

by Michel Hooper-Immins

"Gundry converted an old mill on West Bay Road, whose waterwheel still dips in the River Brit."

KING George III reigned in the year 1794 as Samuel Gundry, a name more famous in Bridport for ropemaking, decided to go into the brewing business.

Gundry converted an old mill on West Bay Road- whose waterwheel still dips in the River Brit- and founded the legendary Bridport Brewery. The thatched brewhouse is largely unaltered today, 221 years later, the oldest in Dorset- producing some 50,000

pints of outstanding Dorset real ale every week.

Eventually, Job Legg took over from Gundry and four years after he died in 1892, his executors sold the business to John Cleeves and Robert Henry Palmer. The Palmer family have been in charge since 1896.

Three masterful portraits hang in the Brewery's boardroom. Great grandfather J. C. Palmer- resplendent in red robes as Mayor of Bridport- and their father Tony Palmer look approvingly over brothers

Fifty thousand pints a week go through the fermenting tanks.

John and Cleeves Palmer, the modern forward-thinking motivators of this flourishing business. With 44 and 34 years service respectively, they are the fourth generation of this most successful of Dorset family businesses, owning all the shares between them. The third portrait is of John Palmer, painted to mark 40 years in the business.

I admire Palmers style and commitment, dedicated to serving superb real ale and distinctive food in their 55 tenanted houses- 39 in West Dorset, ten in Somerset and six in Devon. The tried and tested practice of a brewery with a tenanted estate ensures consistent quality. Employing 49 at the brewery, the business is expanding quietly and organically.

Tally Ho! to '200' and the other ales

I've always been fond of a pint or three of real ale, served in the traditional English way by handpumps and in my view, Palmers slightly vinous 200 ale is quite the best. Launched in 1994 to celebrate the bicentenary of this wonderful thatched brewery on the outskirts of Bridport, 200 strong ale heads the portfolio of six splendid draught beers. Today, they are highly regarded for their flavour and taste.

Brewing- "the fusion of ingredients like malted barley, Kentish hops and yeast with spring water in a sort of giant teapot."

Brewing beer is a skill learnt by years of experience and Darren Batten is at the top of his profession. An age-old process, it is the fusion of ingredients like malted barley, Kentish hops and yeast with spring water in a sort of giant teapot!

A stickler for quality, Darren undertakes informal "quality control" exercises, often calling on Palmers pubs to sample the condition of his beers. He is usually pleased with the result!

Two decades ago, most Palmers beer was sold in their own pubs, but now over 50% is sold to others all over the South and West of England.

Besides my favourite 200 strong ale, Darren Batten brews five other real ales. The most popular is Best Bitter- sometimes called IPA- which accounts for over a third of all beer sales. Relatively new Copper Ale is fruity and malty, now a popular fixture. Strongest is the splendid Tally Ho! -our Dorset Year Book Editor's favourite- now available all year round. This flavoursome nutty brown ale, first brewed in 1949, has many devotees. Lightly hopped Dorset Gold completes the permanent range.

In 2014, Palmers added a sixth brew by producing a seasonal ale for the first time, the "deliciously hoppy" Colmers- named after the iconic tree-topped hill near

Bridport. This was followed by Summer Ale. "There's an incredible array of ale from microbreweries these days," Cleeves Palmer tells me, "and our range had not altered in ten years   We perceive a growing market for lighter and hoppier ales." A third seasonal ale was launched in October 2014.

On a Mission

Finance Director Gary Adcock is a vital part of the board, having been in post for some years. Relatively new to the company is Tenanted Trade Director Jayson Perfect, who joined Palmers last year from London brewer Fullers. His mission is to grow the quality of the pub estate across all areas of activity- from good beer and food

to welcome and service. He has highlighted the increasing interest in social media, encouraging pubs to become involved in sites like Twitter and Facebook.

The estate stretches from rural Piddlehinton in the east to yachty Salcombe in South Devon and north as far as Glastonbury and Bicknoller in the Quantocks. All Palmers houses are individual businesses, supported and encouraged by the brewery, who encourage high standards of food and real ale.

The Palmers management team toast the launch of Colmers seasonal ale, [left to right:]
Chairman John Palmer,
Head Brewer Darren Batten,
Sales & Marketing Director Cleeves Palmer
and Tenanted Trade Director Jayson Perfect.

What a pub crawl

So many public houses in the Palmers estate are real gems. The writer has visited almost every Palmers pub over the years!   One of his favourites is the Anchor Inn at Seatown, in the shadow of Golden Cap and with only the South West Coast Path between the pub and the beach. Palmers have spent over a million pounds to improve the facilities, create a new terrace and add three guest rooms. Paul Wiscombe has run this jewel of a seaside pub for ten years. Dating from 1750, the Anchor Inn is at its most atmospheric on a wild winters day as rain lashes in from the English Channel, but sitting in front of the open fire with a jug of Palmers 200, you are in another world altogether............

In Lyme Regis, veteran landlord Bill Wiscombe- father of Paul- runs the faultless Pilot Boat Inn, at the very centre of the resort. The fish menu covers several blackboards, freshly landed from the iconic Cobb harbour by local fishermen. When HMS

Formidable sank off Lyme on New Years Day 1915, a number of survivors were carried, half dead, into the warmth of the Pilot Boat Inn. Lassie, landlord Tommy Atkins' rough-haired collie, sat beside a sailor given up for dead and licked and warmed him back to life. So was born the Hollywood legend of Lassie.

The atmospheric Anchor Inn at Seatown, in an idyllic coastal location, where over a million pounds has been spent on refurbishment.

You just can't get any nearer to Lyme beach than the terrace of the solidly traditional 400 year old Royal Standard. The back door opens right out onto the sand! The Duke of Monmouth landed just along the beach in 1685. Had he sampled the quality of the food and ale here, might he never have marched off to his eventual execution?

The majority of the Palmers estate is clustered around Bridport and Lyme Regis. The Ropemakers in Bridport's main street reflects the local industry- a town pub of excellence and character. The village pubs show enterprise, attracting customers from all over Dorset. The Loders Arms in Loders village, the Crown at Uploders, the White Horse at Litton Cheney and the Fox & Hounds at Cattistock are all well worth a trip. At the isolated Hare & Hounds at Waytown, the ale is drawn directly from the cask- without the intervention of a pump. Very few Dorset pubs use this delightful method of dispense.

During a holiday in Torquay, the writer found the 15th. century Sea Trout Inn, a relatively new acquisition for Palmers at Staverton Bridge, excelling in every way. Exporting good Dorset ale to Devon's beautiful Dart Valley, we enjoyed two pints of superb 200 strong ale. The menu was so tempting- a choice between whole Torbay plaice in prawn brown butter, poached salmon fillet Nicoise or natural smoked haddock rarebit, chive mash, poached egg and spinach. We chose the latter, a well cooked culinary treat, served with a big smile. An outstanding country pub.

"We are looking to expand our pub estate, to fill in the gaps within 60 miles of the brewery," reveals Cleeves Palmer. "We're proud of our coastal and destination pubs over three counties, keen on the best customer service and training. We strive for high standards."

All Palmers pubs are inspected by Cask Marque, an independent quality inspection service. Palmers new Academy of Beer sets out to give pub tenants and their staff masterclasses in preparing and serving fine ale in tip-top condition. "It's all about our passion as a brewer, about our licensees being proud of our products and about our customers being very discerning," enthuses Head Brewer Darren Batten.

The grape and the grain

I was surprised to discover such a noted real ale business has also been ageing and blending whisky for a hundred years- one of the last brewers still to do so. Branded "Golden Cap," two Scotch whiskies are blended with spring water coming down from the Dorset hills, in old French cognac barrels which date from the early 19th. century. Next to the brewery is Palmers bright Wine Store, which stocks over 900 different wines from around the world and dispenses Palmers draught ales in takeaway carrykegs. One innovation are online sales [www.palmerswinestore.com] where bottled beers, wines, mugs and glasses can be delivered direct to customers anywhere on the UK mainland.

Five per cent of the brewery output is bottled. Ginger Ale and lemonade have been introduced in distinctive tall bottles.

The popular brewery tour starts again at Easter, beginning at the very top of the brewery and walking through the entire process. Telephone 01308 427500 for information.

Cheers! To Charity

Palmers has always been good to local good causes and over five years have donated £30,381 to the Chesil Trust at Portland's National Sailing Academy, helping young or disabled sailors to enjoy the delights of sailing. This sum represents 5p. from the sale of every pint of draught Dorset Gold.

The Palmers Brewery Fund distributes around £10,000 annually to charities and non-political initiatives within a twelve mile radius of Bridport and Lyme Regis. Loders Youth Club received £400 to fund childrens' arts and crafts activities.

Palmers have sponsored the Melplash show for decades- in 2013 Cleeves Palmer became the fourth member of the family to be elected President of the prestigious annual event.

Cleeves Palmer is upbeat about the future- "overall, business is good, the real ale trade is holding steady, the benefit of a decline in lager and stout sales as customers switch to real ale again. There is a welcome move towards local products."

A vital part of any pub's offering is distinctive food. Provenance is vital these days as customers like to know where the ingredients were sourced. Many Palmers pubs display the sources of their food- the name of the farm for meat and eggs for example. There has never been a better time for Dorset food and drink to thrive.

Cleeves Palmer reveals an increasing trend for pubs to grow vegetables and herbs in the pub garden- an incredibly short journey from garden to plate.

The family firm have never become distracted or sidetracked by other business ventures. "We focus only on our core business," says Cleeves Palmer, "concentrating on traditional pubs and brewing good traditional ale."

Because the directors are visible every day, this motivates the workforce, heightening morale. "Palmers is a growing company, because we all put a lot of effort behind it," Cleeves says. "John and I care and because of that, our staff care too."

Five outstanding real ales make up the Palmers range, plus the changing seasonal ales

Managing Director John Palmer has four children, while Sales & Marketing Director Cleeves Palmer has two. There's obviously hope that some of the six siblings will continue this thriving local business into the fifth generation since 1896. Both brothers are longstanding members of The Society of Dorset Men.

Cleeves Palmer jokingly calls the Brewery a "working museum" and a very fine advert for the brewer's craft it is.   I raise my jug of 200 ale to Palmers continued success.

Keeping Alive the History of a family at Sea

Weymouth Merchant Schooners of the 1870's

By Patrick Hodder

IT was normal in the mid to late 1800 s for a businessman with money to invest in the purchase of a sailing vessel. The price was typically split into sixty- four shares and the Ship's Master took ship and cargo to a distant port and traded the cargo for what he could get. If by hard work and good business the Ship's Master prospered, he too could legally purchase shares in the vessel until it became his property. This business was normally transacted by a Ships' Broker.

THE CHIMÆRA of PORTLAND. C. HODDER

One such sailing vessel was a Merchant Schooner called the 'Chimæra' official number 5762, built in Bideford, Devon in 1843. Her construction was of wood with an overall length of 107 feet and a beam of 20 feet. The rigging was as a two-masted topsail schooner and when built had an A1 Lloyds certificate - which meant she had the highest standard of build for that type of vessel. The total volume of her cargo space could hold the equivalent of three to four, forty foot shipping containers. The crew space was in the bow under the main deck, galley was on the main deck aft of the forward mast. The remaining accommodation was at the stern also under the main deck comprising of the Master's cabin, Mate's cabin and a large main cabin which doubled as a mess room and ship's office. Coal stoves were used for heating the living spaces.

Judging by her overall dimensions, it is possible that she was built for the fruit trade that crossed the Atlantic in those days. At one point she sailed out of St Ives, Cornwall to the Mediterranean calling at exotic places like Malta. She ended up sailing out of Weymouth – although it is unclear why.

Whilst based in Weymouth she sailed around the coastal waters picking up and unloading various cargos in such ports as: Antwerp, Dublin, London and the Channel Islands. One such cargo was Portland stone that was used in the construction of many of the great and well-known buildings of Victorian London and Dublin.

Her crew consisted of the Master, the mate, three seamen and one apprentice. All were from the Weymouth and Portland area.

I have a personal interest in this topic as not only did I serve in the Merchant Navy sailing from Weymouth during the 1970s and 80s, but also the Master of the 'Chimæra' was my great- grandfather, Master Mariner Henry Hodder.

He was born 17th April 1827. He first went to sea as an apprentice in 1842 at the age of 15 and gained his Mates certificate in August 1851 at the age of 24. He received his Masters certificate aged 34 in March 1861.

While he was away at sea, the family initially lived with his father-in-law who was the landlord of the George Inn on Weymouth's quay.

The following is taken from the ship's log and gives a flavour of the type of voyages under taken by the 'Chimæra' during a 6- month period in 1874.

Between 1st and 5th January loaded cargo in London. Departed on 6th and arrived at Newport on the 16th January. Discharged and loaded cargo, before leaving for Plymouth on the 28th January. Arriving there 1st February. 16th February departed Plymouth for Portland, arriving there the following day. Departed for Newhaven 21st February, arriving the following day. Returned to Portland 2nd March arriving on the 4th March. Left Portland on 11th March for Dublin arriving 18th March. After unloading and loading, left Dublin on the 31st March for Swansea arriving 7th April. Departed Swansea 16th April for Portland arriving 20th April. Departed Portland 11th May for Dublin arriving 17th May. Departed Dublin 6th June for Swansea arriving 9th June.

<u>Disbursements of the Schooner 'Chimæra' from
23rd November 1870 to 24th March 1871</u>

			£	s	d
Nov	23rd	Custom House charges at Kennetpane		3	6
	25th	Telegraph messages to Dublin		4	3
		Allowance to loaders		<u>7</u>	<u>6</u>
				18	5
Dec	1st	Dublin allowance to pilot		2	0
	7th	Repairing siding lamp etc		2	0
	14th	Shipwrights bill		14	3
		Blacksmiths		14	8
		New rope and canvas as per bill	2	5	3
		2 new charts of Antwerp		8	9
		Block makers	1	5	9
		Allowance discharging cargo		8	9
		" to carpenters		3	9
		" " taking in cargo		5	4
		Present to Deputy Harbour Master		3	0
		Trimmers for trimming 180 of salt rock	1	2	6
		Brokers account	14	6	11
		Help boat out of Dublin 10/- / Present to pilot		<u>11</u>	<u>0</u>
			36	<u>2</u>	<u>11</u>
Jan	4th	Portland Bought off Edward Schollar rope		14	0
		Coal for ships use		<u>4</u>	<u>6</u>
				<u>18</u>	<u>6</u>

Flushing and Antwerp Account from Jan 8th up to March 5th

	£	s	d
Present to pilot at Flushing		1	0
1 Galleon of lamp oil		4	6
2 " " paraffin		5	0
Sundry expenses	1	0	0
Agentsey		10	0
Present to pilot at Antwerp		1	8
½ ton coals at Flushing		12	5
½ ton coals at Antwerp		13	3

			£	s	d
		Ship Chandlers bill		19	4
		Allowance discharging cargo		10	0
		Taking on ballast		5	0
		Brokers account	27	12	6
			32	14	8

Disbursements at West Hartlepool

			£	s	d
Mar	9th	Present to ballast men		2	0
	10th	Dock dues etc	4	11	5
		Ship Chandlers bill		4	7
		2 water breakers repaired		3	0
		Coal fitters account	2	8	2
11th	Trimmers		1	10	0
	Allowance			2	0
		Present to dock gate men		1	0
		" " steam boat men		2	0
		Pilot in and out	10	14	2
May	29th	Bought off Mrs Hone 6 brooms and 2 barge oars		6	6
	30th	Allowance discharging cargo		9	3
		1 man employed at 2d per ton 180 tons	1	10	0
			2	5	9
		Portland Accounts in November 1870		18	5
		Dublin " " December "	36	2	1
		Portland Jan 5th 1871		18	6
		Flushing and Antwerp Account	32	14	2
		West Hartlepool	10	14	2
		Portland Mar 30 / 71	2	5	9
		Total Disbursement	83	13	1
		Total disbursements for the voyage	83	13	1
		Money sent to Mr Scriven	60	0	
		Masters wages for 4 months	28	0	0
		" Voyage money	3	0	0
		Mates wages for 4 months	16	10	0
		Robert Falls	13	0	0
		David Marsh	6	0	0
		Edward Paul	6	0	0
		Antony	6	0	0
		Victualing money	48	0	0
			270	3	1

Dec	12th 1870	Freight received at Dublin 165 tons at 11/3	92	16	3
Mar	1st 1871	" " " Antwerp 182 tons at 11/-	100	11	5
"	28th 1871	" " " Portland 180 tons at 8/-	74	5	0
			267	12	8
		Disbursements	270	3	1
		Balance due to H Hodder	2	10	5
		Paid by Mr Scriven to Mrs Hodder	10	0	0
		" " " " " " Fall	10	15	0
		Cash from Mr Scriven January 4/71	2	0	0
			22	15	0
			2	10	5
		balance due to ship	20	4	7

1871

To insurance fund	43	7	0
Loading expenses at Portland 4 cargoes	43	0	6
Repairs at Guernsey	60	0	0
Sailmakers at Weymouth	36	17	10
Carpenter " "	26	8	5
Smith " "	2	15	1
Anchor and chain	10	0	0
Small items varied	5	9	3
	226	18	10
balance in hand	12	19	3

The Chimæra

1871

Cash received from Captain	239	18	1

To put these figures into some kind of perspective, £1 in 1871 would have had roughly the same buying power as £60 today. A wage of £100 would be equivalent to £60,000 today.

An Untimely End

I have a Bill of Sale for the 'Chimæra' dated 1877. It indicated that, at that time, my great-grandfather had managed to own half of the vessel (ie. 32 shares). So, what became of her?

Under a new owner and Captain, the untimely end of the 'Chimæra' came on the 26th November 1881 whilst on a voyage between Seaham and Shoreham-by-Sea. She was carrying coal at the time. The 'Chimæra' – like all schooners of the time - was not fitted with an engine and so relied on wind and tides to navigate its way. At one point during the journey, the winds picked up to a battering, force 9 gale. The 'Chimæra' was forced to take shelter and anchor off Dungeness (50.56.40N 01E). Tragically, the anchor chain gave way and she was carried out to sea with the loss of two of her crew.

After the 'Chimæra', my great grandfather had already become Master of another merchant schooner called the 'Annie'- official number 74742, built in 1877 in Kingston on Sea, Shoreham, Sussex.

Bills of Sale for the 'Annie' dated 1881 showed that he owned 16 of the 64 shares and in 1884 he had acquired a further 16 shares.

However, fate was not kind to her, as on the 16th January 1886, she was run down in the River Thames of all places - on Bugsby Reach, near Greenwich - by the steam ship 'RECEPTA' of London. This was after having sailed from Guernsey with a cargo of stone and 3 passengers. Luckily there were no fatalities.

Below is a list of Captain Hodder's belongings that went down with the ship – no doubt handed to Lloyds for insurance purposes.

	£	s	d
Watch and chain	8	0	0
2 pairs of binoculars	9	0	0
Sextant	4	4	0
Charts, instruments etc	10	0	0
Barometer	1	10	0
Double gun,2 revolvers etc	0	0	0
Desk	1	0	0
Two suits best cloth cloths	7	15	0
New overcoat	3	5	0
Sea cloths	5	0	0
Underclothing flannels etc	10	0	0
Oil cloths 2 suits	1	5	0
2 pairs sea boots etc	4	0	0
Bed and bedding, cushions etc	7	0	0
Books	1	10	0
China ,cutlery and glass	2	0	0

Tablecloths towels etc	1	0	0
2 looking glasses	1	0	0
3 hats	0	15	0
	88	4	0

Master Mariner Henry Hodder

He left the sea aged 63 and became Deputy Harbourmaster in Weymouth where he became a well-liked and respected figure until his death in May 1904. He was 77.

The Merchant Schooner class went into decline with the growth of the railways, which took most of their general cargo. Some schooners survived until just before WW2 by reducing the sail area and fitting engines.

While researching the subject with such books as, ' Schooner Sunset' by Douglas Bennet, and visits to various museums with their fine ship models, I decided to build an actual working, floating replica of the 'Chimæra'.

A working scale model

It is a scale model as faithful to the original plans and dimensions as I could make it. All of the parts are handmade, not bought from a model shop. The scale is half inch to the foot – the smallest scale to operate the rigging in a realistic manner.

The hull was made in two sections. The top section (see picture above) from main deck up includes rigging and sails which are fully operational. The rigging is operated by hand from a middle deck running the length of the ship. The middle deck also supports the radio controlled steering gear, which is attached to the top section.

The lower section makes up the bulk of the hull and holds the ballast for making the model stable whilst afloat.

Deck furnishings (ie winches, hatches, galley, skylights and holds) are all scratch-built and secondary to the rigging of the model.

If required, all sails can be reduced or lowered depending on the strength and direction of the wind. The model is stable when under full sail in a light wind.

The hull section.

It must have been a magnificent sight to see the Schooners under full sail – although in reality this rarely used to happen because of wind direction and sea conditions.

The Somerset and Dorset Family History Society

40 years on – by Bob Barber, Editor of The Greenwood Tree

2015 marks the 40th anniversary of the Somerset and Dorset Family History Society (SDFHS). The Society was the brainchild of Mervyn Medlycott, who convened a meeting in the village hall at Sandford Orcas in June 1975, following an appeal in the Spring to anyone interested. Some 25 people turned up, from all over Dorset and Somerset, and a committee was formed. G W Squibb QC, an expert in heraldry and Dorset history, was the first President, and Mervyn Medlycott the first Chairman and Secretary. Two well-known names in the field of family history, Donald Steel and David Hawkings, were elected as Vice-Presidents. A number of committee meetings were held during the Summer and a constitution was thrashed out, an advertising brochure produced, a programme of meetings was organised and thought given to the possibility of producing a Society newsletter.

Mervyn - later Sir Mervyn - Medlycott, a professional genealogist who has published widely, took on his present role of President of the Society in 1987. He was elected a Fellow of the Society of Genealogists in 1990.

Rapid growth

The Society was formally launched in Yeovil in September 1975. By November 1975 the membership had reached 86 and grew rapidly, in line with many other family history societies, for many years. This was a boom time for family history; The Federation of Family History Societies (FFHS) had been formed in 1974, and within eighteen months the number of member societies had grown from 7 to over 50. The aims of the SDFHS were, and remain, to advance the education of the public in the study of family history, genealogy and heraldry with particular reference to Somerset & Dorset, and to promote the preservation, security, accessibility and publication of archival material.

Over the years the Society has been active in publishing the works of its members. Census indexes for 1841, 1851 and 1891; databases of baptisms, marriages and burials; a wide variety of name indexes; memorial inscriptions; transcriptions of Dorset and Somerset war memorials; parish register transcriptions and a miscellany of other material has been propagated by a publications sub-committee.

Although the Society has been centred on Sherborne, both geographically and organisationally, there are now ten regional groups that hold meetings locally, usually on a monthly basis. The Blackmore Vale group meets in Sturminster Newton; East Dorset in Wimborne; Mid-Somerset in Street; Sedgmoor in Highbridge; South Dorset in Weymouth; West Dorset in Loders and West Somerset in Alcombe near Minehead. There are also groups based in Frome, Taunton and Yeovil.

A file on every parish

BY the time of its 25th anniversary the Society had over 4000 members and was looking to find a more permanent base from which to run its affairs, having existed in back bedrooms and then on a small industrial estate in Taunton. It occupied the first of its sites in Sherborne in the Glove Factory (now a private house) and then in the basement of the Old Schoolroom in the grounds of the former Congregational Church in Long Street.

The Society moved to its current building on the Parade, at the bottom of Cheap Street in 2006. The Family History Centre, the Society Headquarters, has resources

SDFHS - Family History Centre

and an informed and dedicated group of volunteers on hand to help with family history research at whatever level. The Centre is the first port of call for our many out-of-county and overseas visitors. There is a network of computers with access to the main family history websites, plus much more available on the Internet. We have a file for every parish in Somerset and Dorset and these contain transcriptions of many baptisms, marriages and burials in the Anglican church, as well as similar details for other denominations. The majority of the files also hold memorial inscriptions (MIs) and similar material. There are also 'parish packs' which give additional local information.

The Society Library has over 5,000 family, local, and military history items, as well as CDs, microfiches and maps. These cover a wide range of relevant topics including village histories, areas of specialist research, and the works of many local authors. The collection includes The History of Somersetshire (1791) by the Rev. John Collison and The History and Antiquities of the County of Dorset (1861) by John Hutchins.

Meetings and Courses

The Centre in Sherborne holds regular meetings, including teaching courses for beginners in family history as well as more specialised subjects. Topics covered recently include a conservation workshop, practical sessions on reading old handwriting, the use and dating of photographs in family history, industrial archaeology, and the causes of the First World War, with guidance on tracing WW1 ancestors. The Society is also part of the Sherborne Heritage Alliance.

The Greenwood Tree

The Society's journal was first published as a newsletter in 1975, shortly after the founding of the Society. We have published over 150 editions and the journal has grown to be one of the most respected family history journals anywhere. In 1998, 1999 and 2000 it was joint runner-up in the Elizabeth Simpson competition organised by the FFHS. In 2001 The Greenwood Tree won the Elizabeth Simpson Award outright and won again in 2010 & 2011 in the category for large Societies. It has had a number of editors over the years, most recently Colin Dean, who held the post between 1995 and 2005 and was mainly responsible for quality, style and appearance of the journal, and Chris Storrar who followed as editor for seven years up to the end of 2012.

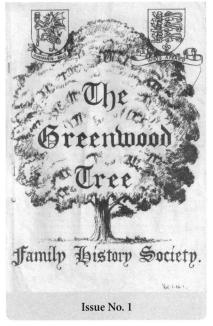

Issue No. 1

The Society has had a website for a number of years, and in recognition of the growing importance of social media, joined Facebook at the end of 2013. More information about the Society and its activities can be found on http://www.sdfhs.org/, with more recent updates on Facebook: https://www.facebook.com/SomersetDorsetFHS.

In line with many other family history societies the SDFHS has struggled with declining membership in recent years. The decline has largely been halted following an energetic programme of activities and advertising the advantage of membership. This, and careful financial management, has set the Society well on track for the next 40 years.

Thanks to Ann-Marie Wilkinson (current Chairman), Ted Udall (Secretary), Iain Swinnerton, Colin Dean, Barry Brock and Delia Horsfall and to the volunteers, too many to mention by name, who have helped the Society through its first 40 years.

A recent cover of The Greenwood Tree

Swanage in The Great War

From tented WWI army camp to prestigious residential estate by Steve White

THE area north of Swanage, before the steep climb up to Ballard Down, is quiet farmland now. . . but 100 years ago thousands of troops were stationed here prior to going off to war. This is the story of the fields around Whitecliffe Farm and their role in the Great War.

Swanage in 1914 was no stranger to visits by the army. For decades the town had hosted tented training camps of 'volunteer' soldiers -now the Territorial Army- from various parts of the country. Training would normally take place every August, on the area beneath Ballard Down. Records go back to as early as the 1860's detailing these camps and the activities that took place.

An idea of what the soldiers did in these tented camps during peacetime training operations can be found in newspaper articles of the time. In the Swanage and Wareham Gazette of August 11 1906 almost two pages are devoted to an article reporting the events of the previous week; under the main heading 'VOLUNTEER CAMP AT SWANAGE' with a sub-heading of '5,000 VOLUNTEERS IN DORSET', it tells of the annual training of the Hampshire Volunteer Brigade, when the 2nd, 3rd, 4th and 5th battalions, camped at Whitecliffe, carried out manoeuvres against a group of other battalions based at Lulworth. It seems the operations continued for most of the week.

Swanage Camp 1908

Such then, were the military exercises that took place annually in Swanage - every summer a huge tented camp appeared, and just as quickly was gone.

The War to end all Wars

Everything changed on 4th August 1914 with the outbreak of the Great War. Swanage was now going to see an unprecedented number of soldiers and horses descend upon the town and these would need to have permanent accommodations; tents were totally inadequate.

The impact upon Swanage was colossal. Over 3600 men camped permanently outside of the town for almost 4 years. Whilst local businesses might have relished this, there were clearly highs and lows for the populace - already affected by the war in Europe.

Again, it's the newspapers that give us a direct link to what it was like to have the army in town. Initially, there seems to have been no restriction upon what could be reported. Readers were told which battalions arrived, from whence they came, their numbers - virtually all there was to know. By early1915 the news items were much less detailed, mundane even, reporting the odd football match or problems caused by individual soldiers in the town. By mid 1915 it appears that restrictions on what could be reported were very tight and not much was said at all.

The first 500 soldiers to arrive in the first days of October 1914 came from Sheffield. Their reception was so warm it seems to have surprised them. Newspapers tell of 'a

View of Camp - January 1915

most enthusiastic welcome, which the men appreciated.' This was short lived. With troops arriving every few days, the novelty soon wore off.

Swanage plays its part

By the beginning of October 1914 the presence of troops in Swanage began to have negative effects on the people of the town. Aside from examples of petty theft carried out by the new arrivals -some troops ended up facing military justice and were subject to court martial- licensing hours were adversely effected. As the following newspaper report tells us - October 7, 1914 -'Early Closing of Publichouses(sic) - with the arrival of the troops which are encamped at Swanage, notification has been given by the police to occupiers of licensed premises that the latter have to be closed by 9 p.m. The same order will be in force in the villages of Studland and Langton Matravers.'

However, it wasn't all negative. October 31 1914 - 'A football match was played at the Recreation Ground on Thursday afternoon between the Swanage Thursday XI and a team chosen from the 232nd Battery R.F.A [Royal Field Artillery] stationed in the town. The latter won by 2 goals to1. Mr A. H. Bartlett was the referee.' And, in the same paper: 'More Troops Arrive. On Thursday afternoon another five hundred men arrived for the camp in Victoria Avenue, whilst four hundred came in yesterday (Friday). Many of them had been drafted from barracks. The men, however, will soon be housed in better quarters, for the building of sheds has been started.'

The last line of the above report gives us a vivid picture of what was happening in Swanage in November and December of 1914. The 'camp' in Victoria Avenue was made up of tents, but work was now underway to build sheds that would become permanent housing -at least until the end of WWI- for the troops. The statement that 'many of the men had been drafted from barracks' tells us that they were coming from 'proper' accommodation to sleep under canvas during the worst weeks of winter.

Forgotten at the Station

The people of the town were no longer meeting the new arrivals at the station, and nor were the military either! A report from November 5 1914 tells of the arrival of 'large drafts' of troops, some having travelled overnight from Glasgow, with little food for the journey, stepping from the train to find nothing organised for their arrival. Standing in the rain they were soaking wet and 'somewhat rowdy'. Arrangements were hurriedly made for them to be given beds in local houses for the night.

Was complacency setting in? The answer was 'probably not'. The people of Swanage, still keen to help where they could, had arranged for meeting places in the town where refreshments could be procured and free paper was on hand so that troops could 'write home' - sales of stamps were enormous. Many picture postcards sent by the troops show Swanage as their origin. Some locals were concerned about the forthcoming festive season. The following plea was made in a column on 10th November by Mr James Day for the townsfolk to allow two or three soldiers - Kitchener's troops as they tended to called- to share Christmas Day with them 'to get them away from the mud and the cold. Some will be in huts by then' he says 'but many will still be in tents'. Another request made in a news column was for Christmas Puddings for the soldiers.

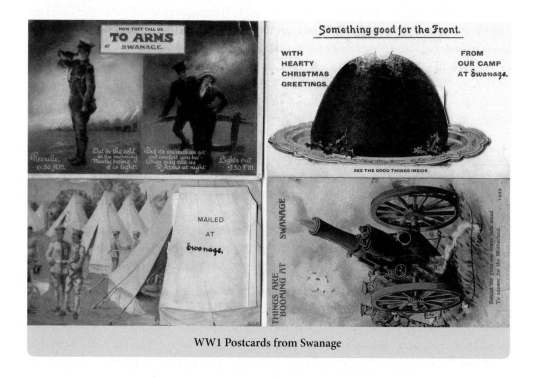

WW1 Postcards from Swanage

A Perfect Sea of Mud

Apparently, from mid October to the end of December 1914 the weather was like last winters - strong winds from the south-west accompanied by cold and rain. The result, inevitably, was a campsite described as a 'perfect sea of mud' due to the clay soils of the area and the large numbers of men traipsing the site. On 12 November 1914 one newspaper claimed of the troops - 'town-bred men, as most of them are, they could not reconcile themselves to the carrying about of enough clay and soil on their boots to make a land tax collector consider whether he could 'levy'! Living in tents in these conditions was clearly not pleasant. Not all troops were under canvass. A good number were given shelter with Swanage residents but they were the lucky few. Many of the others, ironically, considering themselves unfortunate to have to endure such conditions whilst training for war, were destined to end up in far worse conditions - in trenches, facing constant barrages from the enemy.

The building of the new camps must have brought welcome relief and by early 1915 an official photograph taken from Ballard Down shows camp number 1, in what was called the 'Rocket Field', now the Ballard Estate. The camps were built by two local firms - Hardy of Swanage and Parsons & Hayter. The main contractors were MacDonald Gibbs and Co - Consulting Engineers to the War Department. The pictures show their own story.

Horses were still an integral part of the army. The Great War was to become the first 'mechanised war' and was effectively the last time horses were used in battle. It is interesting to note that the original plight and subsequent improvement of the condition of these animals was noted in March 1915 - 'General training has been the routine of the week, and this embraces a great variety of duties. The horses are daily exercised, and so are the mules, and both species show the change that attention and good feeding have worked in them since they arrived, many in poor condition, some few weeks ago. The men are becoming expert riders, and we understand that some animals are already undergoing training as gun teams.'

Kitted out for Mesopotamia - 2 July 1916

The pressing needs of the army meant the usual planning processes were largely ignored. At a meeting of the Works Committee the Surveyor reported that there were several matters which should be given his attention. The Chairman of the Council and the Clerk arranged an interview with a 'General Purvis' to propose the camp should be in another place. The reply was that the camp was too far advanced to be altered. The council's main objection was sanitation. They were informed that a sewer that had been laid would carry only cook-house water into the sea and that alternative arrangements would be made for sewage.

Many regiments were stationed in Swanage during WWI, including Reserve Battalions of the East Lancashire Regiment, Reserve Battalions of the Worcester Regiment and 9th Reserve Battalion of the Somerset Light Infantry.

Despite the fact that the troops stationed in Swanage, and other parts of Dorset, were essentially here for training, there were still deaths reported. A small entry into a local paper on 25 February 1915 tells of the death on 21st February of Percy William Scott, Gunner, R.F.A (Royal Field Artillery) aged 24 years. The paper says; 'A firing party fired the usual three volleys over the open grave, and the trumpeters sounded the 'Last Post'. How he died is not explained.

The Petty Sessions column of 25th March 1915 gives two instances of the troops' getting their 'collars felt'. Two soldiers of the R.F.A were caught taking a bag of coal and coke from the council yard. Owing to the fact that they had only been in the town for a month and had 'excellent characters," they were bound over under the 'First Offenders Act' and had to pay costs of 6s.6d.

The same article mentions two other soldiers of the R.F.A who had stolen a 'quantity of harness'- the property of H.M. Secretary of State for War. After the case was called the Bench were informed that 'the military authorities wished the men handed over to them for court martial, and this was accordingly done'.

Skinny Dipping!

An exchange of letters between the military and Swanage Urban District Council in June 1915 gives us a flavour of local issues causing consternation. Every morning between 5 and 6am the troops would bathe in the portion of Swanage Bay, north of the camp. A letter from the council was written requesting that orders should be given prohibiting the men of the battalion bathing 'without bathing drawers'. Major Charles Lewis of 13th Battalion, Royal Warwickshire Regiment, replied, "I regret that I cannot comply with the request to stop the men bathing unless they wear drawers as these are not supplied by the Authorities and it is certainly necessary and proper that the men should bathe frequently."

Looking back at the time of the Great War when Swanage hosted the camps under Ballard Down, a positive relationship prevailed between the local population and the military, probably because the brave soldiers, training to fight against the enemy overseas, were appreciated by those who lived nearby.

A return to peacetime

The Ballard Estate in Swanage, now a collection of bungalows sitting on the edge of the cliffs overlooking Swanage Bay to the Isle of Wight, occupies an idyllic location. This was just one of the five camps of 'Kitchener's Army' in Swanage. Whilst many have been completely rebuilt, a few of these 'bungalows' are essentially the huts that were constructed in late 1914 and early 1915. A couple still look externally much as they would have, while others have added cladding to disguise their origin.

After the Great War building materials were in very short supply. An auction was held in September 1920 when many of the buildings built for the military were sold off. Apart from the huts built to house the soldiers, there were 80 foot long buildings, clad in corrugated iron, in which the horses had been kept. Latrine blocks, blacksmiths buildings, kitchen blocks and many other buildings associated with the running of a number of army camps. There was also a hospital. It seems that the auction, in the main, was set-up with the buyer having a time limit of 28 days to remove their purchase from the site, leaving the site predominately farmland. The exception was the Ballard Estate. Here the huts were sold where they stood, prior to the auction. This is confirmed in the Swanage Times of 18 September 1920 which states; 'One of the camps has been bought as it stands and is likely soon to be converted into bungalows. It is in a good position on the cliff, overlooking the sea, and should be a big attraction, specially in the season.'

A very early plan was put forward by George Hardy the builder, for the 'Sunshine Estate', although this seems to have been dropped almost immediately. The site was bought in a joint venture between Hardy and another local building company, Pond &Walton, being sold off as individual plots soon after.

By 1915 there had been over 200 buildings among the five camps under Ballard Down, but the 1926 Ordnance Survey map shows less than a dozen buildings remaining. Today, some of the concrete bases laid for these structures can still be seen in fields around the area. Council records show huts, or bungalows as they were now being called, were already being bought privately in 1921. They each had a rateable value of £17.

Six of the huts were procured by the Holiday Fellowship, set up in 1913 by T A Leonard, designed to allow people of similar interests to share walking holidays. These were named after parts of the Lake District, where the organisation had its first properties. A further two huts were added to the portfolio soon after. Photos from

Holiday Fellowship at Swanage 1926

this time show Fellowship members, who had spent a week or two walking the area, posing outside one of the huts. By 1934 the huts had been sold off and a building purchased in the town for their holiday groups, this too has since been sold. The Holiday Fellowship still exists as HF holidays, and has a large number of premises around the country, including one at Lulworth Cove.

Since the sale of the huts on the popular Ballard Estate in the 1920's, many owners have come and gone. Recently one bungalow was on sale at £825,000 while another two-bedroom bungalow was for sale by tender with a guide price of £600,000. How many of those troops, sleeping 30-40 per hut, could have imagined that?

Thanks to Hillary Passmore and David Haysom at Swanage Museum for their invaluable help in compiling this article.

The Collingwoods Remembered

by Chairman of the Society of Dorset Men - Stuart Adam

ON 5th June, "The Friends of the Collingwood Memorial" will hold a special service to remember the Officers and Men of the Collingwood Battalion (RND) who fell on this day one hundred years ago in the Battle of Krithia, during the Dardanelles Campaign, the final attack against Ottoman defences on the Gallipoli peninsula.

An annual service has been organised to commemorate the event since 1919, firstly by my Grandfather, Frederick Adam, then by my father Roy and, since 2008, by me.

The Collingwoods, one of eight battalions of the Royal Naval Division named after famous admirals or ships, derived their title from Admiral Lord Cuthbert Collingwood whose naval career, spanning the American War of Independence and Napoleonic War, was marked by a number of victorious encounters. It was as Nelson's second-in-command at the Battle of Trafalgar that Collingwood achieved his greatest notoriety,

both as Master of the ship Royal Sovereign and by taking command of the battle on the death of Nelson. His statue overlooking the river and sea at Tynemouth provides a Dorset connection. It was sculpted by John Graham Lough from Portland stone.

The Collingwood Battalion completed wartime training at Blandford Camp under it's commanding officer, Commander Alexander Spearman, a 53 year old who had seen service in the Royal Navy and retired in 1906. He volunteered for active service at the outbreak of war and was appointed to the Royal Naval Division. His adjutant was Lt. Cmdr. Wallis Noir Annand, aged 28, whose son, born after his father's death, won a VC in the Second World War.

Leaving Blandford on 10th May 1915, the Collingwood Battalion arrived at Cape Helles on the Gallipoli Peninsula on 29th May and advanced to the front line, less than four miles away, by 1.30am on Friday 4th June. The plan was to leave their support trench at noon, group into a firing line and 'go over the top' at 2.15pm. The violent bombardment by the British artillery and the naval fleet against enemy positions ceased at 11.30 so the Collingwood firing line made a feint, brandishing bayonets and cheering, to entice the Turkish Reserves to action. The bombardment recommenced and at noon the CO and his adjutant lead the attack. Commander Spearman was wounded in the leg but, undaunted, he rose, took off and waved his cap, brandished his revolver and shouted "Come on Collingwoods, don't leave me now." He was killed instantly with a shot through the head.   Lt. Cmdr. Annand was also killed. Although suffering heavy losses the Collingwoods advanced a distance of 400 yards to the Turkish trenches but, owing to the French soldiers on either side of their position retreating, found themselves surrounded and forced to retire.

In the space of half an hour 16 Collingwood officers were killed or missing, eight wounded and there were over 500 casualties among the men. On this fateful and tragic day 55 of the 64 RND officers were killed or wounded.

On the night of June 5th, having rallied in the support trenches under the command of the only two surviving officers, the Collingwoods were relieved. The men were dispersed among other units and from 8th June 1915 the Collingwood Battalion ceased to exist. They were in existence for such a short time a cap badge was never produced.

I actually met one of the surviving officers, Sub.Lieut. Arthur Watts, who had been wounded whilst attempting to supply ammunition to the front line. He subsequently had his right leg amputated. Of the three men assisting him, two were killed outright and the third died of wounds a few days later.

Mustafa Kemal Ataturk (1881-1938) – army officer, revolutionary statesman, founder and first President of the Republic of Turkey – said: "Those heroes who shed their blood and lost their lives are now lying in the soil of a friendly country, therefore Rest in Peace. There is no difference between the 'Johnnies' and the ' Mehmets' to us here – they lie side by side here in this country of ours. You, the Mothers who sent their sons from far away countries, wipe away your tears. Your sons are now lying in our bosom and are in peace. After having lost their lives on this land, they will become our sons as well."

Courtesy of Carolynn Langley
Roll-of-Honour.com

The Collingwood Battalion War Memorial at Collingwood Corner - on the Blandford Forum to Salisbury road - was Grade II listed on 8 July 2014. It was unveiled on 7th June 1919 and overlooks the grounds over which the Royal Naval Division carried out its training.

The giving keeps going

Andy Prowse, Chairman of the Society's Charity Sub-Committee, reports...

THE Society of Dorset Men has continued over the past year to make donations to Dorset based charities.

The Dorset ME Support Group was granted £300 towards invaluable work with victims of this extremely debilitating disease, sometimes known as Chronic Fatigue Syndrome. It affects children as well as adults and can be triggered by a virus, infection, stress or severe exhaustion.

MOSAIC was another worthwhile organisation to benefit from a £300 donation. Based at Milborne St. Andrew, Mosaic offers a pathway of support and guidance for bereaved children, young people and families. Each year 24,000 children in the UK suffer the loss of a parent, sibling or other close relative, shattering, and bringing about big changes in their lives.

Each year the Society donates £100 to the Dorset Echo Toy Appeal.

The Airborne Initiative is also supported. This was set up to 'Challenge Offending Behaviour' by working with staff at Portland Young Offenders Institute to provide five-day courses designed to challenge young offenders to achieve personal success – whether working in a team, learning to understand other's needs or by being placed outside their comfort zone and being helped to react in a motivated and correct manner.

The Chesil Trust is a registered charity dedicated to helping young or disabled people experience water sports, especially sailing and windsurfing. Working with local special schools and adult groups, around 150 people are supported through a special programme for people with disabilities. The Society has donated £300 to provide urgently needed large buoyancy aids.

left to right: Peter Fry, Andrew Prowse, Hugh de Iongh (Chairman - Chesil Sailability), Jane Buckle, Kirsty Lydeard, Anya de Iongh.

A *detailed history for the railway history enthusiast specially produced to mark the 150TH ANNIVERSARY of the PORTLAND BRANCH RAILWAY*

by transport enthusiast, railway historian and author Brian L Jackson

ALTHOUGH the railway eventually reached Weymouth in January 1857 there had been little progress with a line to the island where the stone industry and the evolving naval base awaited rail connection. Eventually a local company the Weymouth & Portland Railway was formed receiving its Act of Parliament in June 1862, as the line was to be operated jointly by both the Great Western Railway and the London & South Western Railway the track as with the main line between Dorchester Junction and Weymouth had to be mixed gauge, the standard 4ft 8½ inch gauge and the then 7ft¼ inch gauge of the GWR. Construction commencing later in the year on the 4 mile 25 chain mile line which started at a junction north of Weymouth station and terminated in Victoria Square at Portland, a long siding extended to Castletown where transfer facilities were made with the Merchants Railway, enabling stone to be conveyed by rail nationwide. Completed in May 1864 unfortunately there were a number of both technical and political difficulties, the branch eventually opening to goods traffic on 9th October 1865, and Monday 16th October saw L.S.W.R. 2-4-0 Well Tank No. 154 Nile haul the first passenger train.

In June 1870 an intermediate station was opened at Rodwell to serve a developing suburb of Weymouth, in June 1874 the broad gauge was removed from the Wilts, Somerset & Weymouth line and the Portland branch, thus removing many of the complications of mixed gauge operation. It was not until 1877 that the naval base was connected by a line from Castletown enabling coal to be brought direct to the Breakwater coal store by rail.

During this time a further scheme had been developing on the island, "The Easton & Church Hope Railway" had been formed in July 1867 to construct a tramway from Inmosthay quarries, north of Easton to Church Ope Cove via an incline to a pier in the cove. Almost a nonstarter from the beginning, it was decided to cut their losses and construct a steeply graded standard gauge line from Easton around the east side of the island to join the Admiralty Railway near the Breakwater and obtain running powers

From top left- clockwise: Rodwell Station, Rodwell Station viewed from Wyke Road Bridge, to Weymouth from Sandsfoot Castle Halt, about to depart from Easton Station, Westham Halt (bottom right,) Melcombe Regis Station in 1909, Easton Station in 1951

over a 24 chain section to join the Portland Railway at Castletown.   However, financial difficulties and other problems it was to take over 35 years and nine Acts of Parliament with extensions of time to construct 3 miles 39 chains, surely a record for a line of such moderate length before the line opened to goods traffic only in 1900 having failed the Board of Trade inspection to carry passenger traffic resulting in further work before the first passenger train arrived at Easton on 1st September 1902.

The opening of the extension to the Breakwater and increasing traffic over the branch required its up grading from a basic single line operated by a Train Staff to a fully signalled railway with a signal box opening at Portland in July 1877, and in December 1892 an intermediate signal box was provided at Rodwell, (although not a passing loop), with the platform extended two years later. The construction of the Whitehead Torpedo factory at Wyke Regis in 1891 required the provision of a siding to serve the establishment, and the nearby original timber viaduct across the Fleet was replaced by a steel structure during 1902. The opening of the Easton extension to passenger traffic saw the opening of a temporary station near the original Portland station in Victoria Square to handle the Easton traffic, passengers having to change trains and walk a short distance between the stations until a new station was constructed on the curve complete with two signal boxes to control the enlarged layout opening in May 1905, the original Portland station becoming a goods depot.

Increased traffic saw Rodwell reconstructed during 1908 with a passing loop, up and down platforms and a new signal box, thus allowing a 50% increase in train capacity. Further improvements followed with the replacement of the timber viaduct over the Backwater with a shorter steel structure with infilling at the Weymouth station end allowing the construction of a new station named Melcombe Regis with passengers making the short walk thus ending the necessity of trains shunting in and out of Weymouth station, these works being completed during 1909. July of the same year saw halts open at both Westham and Wyke Regis, the latter adjacent to the Whiteheads factory although a considerable distance from the Wyke Regis of that time which ended just beyond Wyke Hotel. By this time traffic over the branch had reached a new peak, the stone industry, the Navy, Army and Prison all providing trade. However, the latter three were carried at reduced Government rates which reflected upon branch revenue which caused concern to the railway companies as early as 1908.

The commencement of the First World War saw additional pressure on the branch, there was a constant flow of both naval personal and troops to and from the island. A temporary signal box to assist shunting operations was erected in March 1916 near the later Mere Road crossing, a halt was constructed adjacent to the Naval Hospital for the use of ambulance trains, and pages of instructions issued for the working of ambulance trains into the dockyard.

Following the war the monopoly of the railway was usurped as motor vehicles took to the road, motor buses from Weymouth reached Victoria Square in July 1921 and Tophill by February 1927, the latter providing a superior service to the district much of which was a distance from Portland and Easton station, likewise at Weymouth, Melcombe Regis station was a distance from the town centre which the buses passed through again giving the buses an advantage. In August 1932 Sandsfoot Castle Halt opened to serve the nearby Sandsfoot Castle and gardens, also the new adjacent Southlands housing estate. However, in June 1939 the Southern National Bus Company introduced a service to the estate. Interestingly, the Railways had in the late 1920s acquired a substantial financial involvement in Southern National which gave them a degree of influence in their operations and a share of the profits, a clear case of if you cannot beat them, join them.

During October 1935 advances in signalling allowed the replacement of the two signal boxes that controlled Portland station, "Portland Goods Junction Signal Box" situated half way along the oil tanks, and "Portland Station Signal Box" at the Easton end of the station by one box situated to the Weymouth side of the station.

With the outbreak of war in 1939 the branch became a valuable asset to the war machine, with additional goods traffic and both naval and army specials, and general passenger traffic increased with petrol rationing and reduced bus services. A major threat was attack by air, in all there were thirteen strikes on the branch. A direct hit destroyed the signal box and killed the signalman at Portland on 11th June 1940. In August 1940 a raid severed the Easton line just on the Easton side of the junction of the line into the dockyard, fortunately the junction was not damaged, the Easton section remaining closed for a considerable time. A further raid destroyed the main station building at Rodwell on 15th April 1941 resulting in the death of the porter in charge. A raid on Weymouth on the night of 4th May 1941 resulted in the two sets of passenger stock used on the branch being destroyed whilst berthed at Weymouth Junction. Other raids were mainly near misses, bomb craters and unexploded bombs that causing disruption to services. During the build up to D Day vast amounts of military traffic converged on Portland it was necessary to make alternative arrangements in case the road bridge over the Fleet was attacked for traffic to use the railway bridge, this was achieved by constructing a temporary road from the Portland Road across the site of the present Downclose Estate then to run on the seaward side of the railway line past Wyke Regis Halt before crossing the railway bridge on level crossing type decking before joining a further temporary road to join Beach Road, fortunately this was never put to the test

Following hostilities traffic slowly returned to normal levels although there was a rise in stone traffic owing to a nationwide rebuilding programme, with the continuance of petrol rationing there was little increase in private motoring also bus and road haulage services were constrained. Since the outbreak of war the Railways had been under Government control, on 1st January 1948 the railways were nationalised beginning a new chapter in transport history. Petrol rationing ended in May 1950 resulting in improved bus services and an increase in private motoring, the Portland branch had become unviable and could be served more efficiently by an improved bus service this resulting in its closure to passenger traffic from 3rd March 1952. Goods traffic continued still carrying a considerable amount of stone traffic and naval stores, from the late 1950s an additional traffic was the sending of truck loads of Channel Island traffic to Portland goods shed for checking before transfer to Weymouth Quay for shipment. There had also been a number of special passenger trains over the branch ranging from naval specials, quarrymen's excursions, a number of railway enthusiast railtours, and the Royal Train. Reductions in the Navy saw a decrease in Dockyard traffic, relaxations in road haulage regulations allowed the transportation of stone traffic direct to construction sites. These factors combined with the consequences of Beeching saw the branch close to all traffic after 9th April 1965, when Ivatt 2MT 2-6-2 tank No. 41294 cleared the last wagons from Sheepcroft coal siding at Easton and Whiteheads siding at Wyke Regis.

Within nine years the track, viaducts and other structures had been removed, the site of Easton station was developed as sheltered housing. The track bed between Melcombe Regis station and Ferrybridge was acquired by Weymouth & Portland Council and the two miles section between the former Westham Halt and Ferrybridge transformed into the Rodwell Trail a footpath and cycleway, en route the platforms of Westham Halt, Rodwell Station and Wyke Regis Halt are passed. Today the Rodwell Trail is an integral part of Weymouth life.

27th March 1965 – the last passenger train leaves the remains of Portland Station

The Horse with the Red Umbrella

How historically theatrical ! - John Travell reveals a fascinating story

THIS popular and curiously named cafe in Dorchester, situated on the corner of Trinity Street and High West Street and immediately opposite the Holy Trinity Church, has recently placed a prominent display on view to its customers, presenting the history of the building. This once contained a theatre and had links with the actor Edmund Kean and also with Thomas Hardy.

Kean as Shylock in 1814

Edmund Kean, who went on to become famous as the greatest tragedian of his day, and in the opinion of The Times theatre critic Benedict Nightingale was probably the greatest ever English actor, was born the illegitimate son of a part-time actress and prostitute, in Gray's Inn, London, on 4th November 1787. His maternal grandfather was the playwright, Henry Carey, who was himself the illegitimate son of George Savile, the Marquis of Halifax.

By Royal Command

Kean, whose childhood was very harsh and uncaring, made his first appearance on stage, aged four, as Cupid in Jean-Georges Noverre's ballet of Cymon. When he was 14 he obtained an engagement to play leading parts for twenty nights in the York Theatre, appearing as Hamlet, Hastings and Cato. He then joined Richardson's travelling theatre company, when accounts of his abilities reached King George III, who commanded him to perform at Windsor Castle.

Kean went on to join Saunders' circus, where he suffered a serious accident. He fell off a horse and broke both his legs, leaving him with painful swellings in his feet which affected him for the rest of his life. In 1807 he played leading parts in the Belfast Theatre with the famous actress Sarah Siddons, who regarded him as 'a horrid little man' but found that 'he played very, very well', although 'there was too little of him to make a great actor.' In 1808 he joined Samuel Butler's provincial troupe and then married Mary Chambers of Waterford, the leading actress, who bore him two sons, one of whom became the actor Charles Kean.

A walk to Dorchester and an appointment with fate

In 1813, Kean was appearing in Teignmouth where he was seen by Dr. Drury, the Headmaster of Harrow School, who promised to recommend him to Mr. Pascoe Grenfell and the committee of the Drury Lane Theatre in London. In the meantime Kean had accepted two engagements in Barnstaple and Dorchester from Henry Lee, a well-known theatre manager and impresario.

Being very short of money, Kean walked from Barnstaple into Dorchester carrying his four year-old son Charles on his back, while his wife followed in a post-chaise with their seriously ill son Howard.

The first theatre on the site in Trinity Street had been built for Henry Lee in 1792 by Charles Curme, the architect son of a local builder, and it would have been here that Kean made his life-changing appearance in November 1813.

Although the theatre was only a third full when he made his entrance, sitting alone in a stage box was S.J. Arnold, the Manager of Drury Lane, who had come from London to see Kean for himself. Arnold immediately engaged Kean to appear at Drury Lane on a three-year contract.

Sadly, on 23 November, Kean's son Howard died of measles. He was buried in the Holy Trinity churchyard just across the road from the theatre. The doctor's bill and cost of the funeral left Kean completely without funds, so he acted for a few more days in Lee's theatre and Lee advanced him five pounds to enable him to go to London and start his career at Drury Lane.

His first appearance, in January 1814, as Shylock in The Merchant of Venice was an overnight sensation, and he went on to play the great Shakespearean roles of Othello and Richard III. Kean's career took off and he became very rich, but rapidly lost his wealth in lavish and dissolute living.

Dorchester - Alderman Cox cuckolded

He gained a bad reputation and finally lost all public respect when he was sued for adultery in 1825 with the wife of Alderman Cox, a prominent Dorchester citizen. Kean was ordered to pay the deceived husband £800.

Kean's career collapsed and he died in poverty in 1833. His son Charles went on to have a highly successful and much longer career than his father at Drury Lane's rival theatre of Covent Garden.

A new theatre for Dorchester

Charles Curme built a new theatre for Henry Lee incorporating parts of the fabric of the earlier building. Known simply as The Dorchester Theatre, it was opened on 25 February 1828 with Lee's company presenting performances three times a week.

It became known as the Loyalty until finally closing in 1843 when the building was taken over by Godwin's Glass and China Stores and the theatre used as a warehouse at the back of the shop. The theatre structure remained intact until the building was sold in 1963 and was finally demolished in 1965. The High West Street frontage of the building which still survives became a cafe in 1970.

The Horse with the Red Umbrella is thought to have been the title of one of the plays performed in the theatre.

Thomas Hardy took a great interest in the history of the Dorchester theatres, and in 1897 had written three letters to the Dorset County Chronicle about them and the association with Edmund Kean. In 1924, when the Hardy Players were performing their production of Hardy's own stage adaptation of Tess of the d'Urbervilles,

attracting many visitors to Dorchester, John Godwin opened the theatre to the public. Hardy brought several of his famous guests to see the building. They all signed Godwin's visitors' book which is now in the County Museum. Hardy himself wrote the introduction to the book and among the signatures are those of the playwright and director Harley Granville-Barker, the author of Peter Pan - Sir James Barrie, Sir Sidney Cockerell - the Director of the Fitzwilliam Museum in Cambridge, and the legendary 'Lawrence of Arabia'. At that time Lawrence was living as a private in the Tank Corps under the name 'T.E.Shaw' and always signed himself as 'Shaw'- which he had done in Winston Churchill's visitors' book at Chartwell. But Hardy always knew him as Lawrence and that is the way he signed himself in Godwin's book, probably because Hardy was standing beside him as he wrote. This late signature of his is unusual and rare. The display in The Horse with the Red Umbrella includes a photographic enlargement of the signatures in Godwin's book.

Note: the main sources. Ann Sheridan's 'Circuit theatres in Dorchester and Bridport 1793-1843'. Theatre Notebook 53 (1) (1999) 19-40 in the County Museum. Thomas Hardy's Facts Notebook pps. 324-330.

William Barnes Society

Its aims, campaigns and events – by Society Chairman, Dr. Alan Chedzoy

THE aim of the William Barnes Society is to 'enable its members to share fellowship and pleasure in the life and work of William Barnes'. Its members include scholars and laymen, those chiefly interested in his poetry and others who are drawn by his connection with Dorset history and dialect. In practice it is a group of friends but definitely not a clique. All are made welcome. As the novelist E.M Forster wrote: 'To read Barnes is to enter a friendly cottage where a family party is in full swing..(one which) 'welcomes the entire human race'.

The Society is not normally a campaigning one but became so recently when the West Dorset District Council announced that it was proposing to build 1,000 houses on farmland to the south east of Dorchester, sometimes referred to as 'Came View'.

Winterborne Came Rectory

This is the very land that links Thomas Hardy's home at Max Gate, and William Barnes's Rectory at Winterborne Came. The Chairman of the Society at once wrote a letter, countersigned by the Secretary of the Thomas Hardy Society, which was sent to every member of the West Dorset District Council, protesting at the proposal.

Councillors were reminded that it was through these fields that Thomas Hardy walked on his way to the little church at Winterborne Came, where William Barnes's funeral took place, a walk which Hardy later commemorated in his poem: The Last Signal. The letter pointed out that this section of the 'Hardy Country' was probably the most famous site in the County and one which, through literature, is familiar to people all over the world. It is why the County is famous. Many others joined in the protest, and the President of the William Barnes Society, who is also President of the Campaign to Protect Rural England, Sir Andrew Motion, expressed his disapproval of the scheme in The Times. 'I think this is a really crucial moment', he said, 'We are going to end up with a less beautiful country'. In the event, the proposal was defeated in Council, but there is still every reason cause to keep a watchful eye on any further such schemes.

Meanwhile, the present owner of Willam Barnes's Rectory at Winterborne Came, Mr Warren Davis, had arranged for a small memorial plaque to be placed on the wall facing the garden that the poet loved to tend. This was unveiled by the Chairman of the Society in August last. The plaque reads;

> **The Dorset Poet**
> **William Barnes,**
> **Lived here**
> **1862-1886**

The event was covered in various newspapers including a double-page spread in West Country Life. Further memorials are planned in the form of wooden seats, set with brass plaques, at various sites round the County associated with the poet.

Giles Dugdale

A major initiative of the Dorset County Museum this year has been the purchase of a splendid portrait of Giles Dugdale by Wilfred De Glehn (pictured). Dugdale was a biographer of William Barnes, his book William Barnes Of Dorset coming out in 1953, when it may be said, that the reputation of the poet had almost faded. Dugdale is buried where he lived, in Corfe Castle. The Society made a contribution to this purchase, and several anonymous members also donated a significant sum. Our member, Marion Tait helped to organise a sale in Dorchester to raise funds both for this and for the refurbishment of the Barnes collection and display at the museum. Our treasurer, Brian Caddy, has been fortunate enough to purchase Dugdale's own copy of Lucy Baxter's The Life of William Barnes (1887) together with some pages of hand-written notes. Lucy Baxter (pen name 'Leader Scott') was the daughter of Barnes, and Dugdale made extensive use of her book in writing his own. This too will be presented to the Museum.

In another intitative, the Society has funded two lines from Barnes to be inscribed on the moulding of the ceiling in the County Museum. They are from My Orcha'd in Linden Lea and read:

Wi fruit vor me, the apple tree

Do lean down low in Linden Lea

It will be impossible for any visitor to Dorset to have a cup of tea there without having heard of William Barnes.

One of our indefatigable Barnes evangelists has been Professor Tom Burton of the University of Adelaide. With a colleague, K.K.Ruthven, he has now edited the first volume of The Complete Poems of William Barnes, brought out by the Oxford University Press. Two more volumes are to follow. The Oxford imprimatur once and for all established Barnes as a poet of national—some would say of international—significance. Meanwhile, in his sabbatical year at Cambridge, Tom has been reading and presenting the Dorset poems to audiences at a variety of education institutions, including Cambridge and Aberdeen universities, London drama schools, and Wellington, Winchester and Eton colleges.

Society events this year have included the ever-popular members' evening, organised by Barbara Whillock of Lytton Cheney, in which members' read their favourite poems. In March, Dr. Peter Robson lectured on Barnes and Dorset Folklore, discussing such customs as wassailing, the mummers, lent crocking, the 'evil eye', and so on. As a Christian, Barnes was not a believer in many of these beliefs, but understood their cultural value. The annual service of remembrance is held at Winterborne Came Church every year, which is specially opened for us. The church is set way out in the fields, and is little known even by many Dorset people. This year's service in April was especially memorable for the singing of Linden Lea, by Roma Loukes, a distinguished young opera singer, trained in Sweden, a daughter of one of our committee. The annual summer lunch was addressed by Bonny Sartin, of Yetties fame, who under the title of 'Barnes and Me' told us about his experiences in presenting Barnes' poems and songs around the county and beyond. Bonny was particularly pleased to renew his acquaintance with another member, Jim Potts OBE, who, as an officer of the British Council, had booked him to give performances in many countries round the world. This meeting of old friends is very much in the warm spirited tradition of the poet. The annual visit this year was to the Old Rectory, Winterborne Came (pictured) Barnes's home for twenty-four years.

At the Annual general Meeting the following were elected:

President, Sir Andrew Motion; Vice-Presidents, Warren Davis, Tim Laycock; Chairman, Dr. Alan Chedzoy; Vice-Chair and Hon. Treasurer, Brian Caddy; Secretary, Jill Bryant; Committee, David Downton, Rod Drew, Christopher Heath,

Audrey Loukes, Peter Metcalf, Marion Tait, and Helen Gibson (co-opted as a link with the Thomas Hardy Society).

Guests are always welcome at our meetings. Applications for membership and any enquiries should be directed to: Brian Caddy, 31 Casterbridge Road, Dorchest, DT1 2AH, tel. 01305 260348

Meetings are usually held at the Dorford Centre, Top o' Town, Dorchester, at 7pm for 7.30.

William Barnes statue

WARMEST thanks and appreciation are expressed to all who have supported the production of this Year Book and for the co-operation of Contributors, particularly those whose submissions were unable to be included. Every care has been exercised to ensure the appropriate acknowledgement of articles, poetry and illustrations has been given to copyright holders. If omission has inadvertently occurred, apologies are tendered with a request for the owner's kind and courteous indulgence. - Editor

DORSET PLACE NAMES

A tour of the county in poetry by Eric Gosney

If you really know your Shakespeare

You'll recall some words of fame

When in 'Romeo and Juliet' she remarks,

"What's in a name ?" . . . .

But I'm thinking now of Dorset,

whilst at county maps I stare

and confess I'm fascinated

by the names encountered there.

I was born and bred in Dorset

and I love its countryside.

O'er the years I have explored it

Both on foot and cycle ride.

But one can't know every corner

As I'm sure you will agree

And some places in the County

Are just names on maps to me.

There are royal links in Dorset!

Tollard Royal and quiet Kingstag

Melcombe, Lyme and heath-girt Bere

All bear the Royal 'Regis' tag.

Family names occur quite widely –

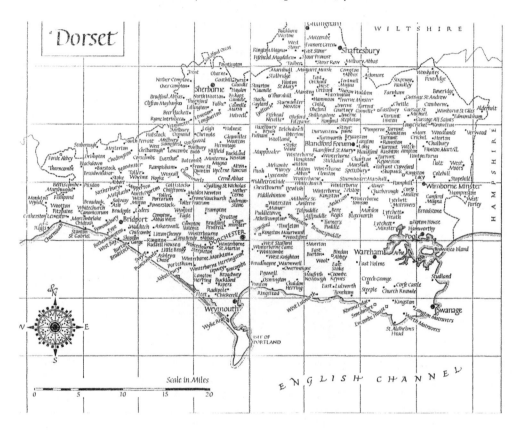

Melbury Osmond, Sampford, Bubb-

Glanville's Wootton, Okeford Fitzpaine,

Melcombe Bingham's in that club.

Streams and rivers name some places

Sturminster on Stour lies

Then the River Bride marks Bridport

Weymouth causes no surprise.

There are 'puddles' and some 'piddles'

Kiddle's Bottom sounds quite rude!

Shitterton, by local ladies in Bere Regis, is eschewed !

Saints abound, denoting churches – Gussage, Sydling, Milborne too.

Winterbournes are ten-a-penny; Tarrants, Iwernes – quite a few.

Ryme Intrinsica's mysterious – Dorchester where Romans came.

Toller Fratrum and Porcorum, Blandford Forum – Latin name ?

There are names I find delightful - Melplash, Mappowder and Plush

If you're out and need refreshment try the local pubs – they're lush !

Tincleton sounds quite melodic – Fiddleford sounds much the same

Rampisham sounds rough-and-ready   and   Beer Hacket "Frightful name !"

Where's the smallest pub in Dorset ? Can you Cross-in-Hand locate?

Have you seen God's Blessing Green ? Admired the view from Dagger's Gate ?

Llew Powys lived in Chaldon Herring, but where is his memorial stone ?

Witchampton's a spooky place, so don't explore it on your own !

I must end this brief collation for you're clearly quite punch-drunk !

But I hope this peroration – in your mind and heart – has sunk.

Take a trip in Dorset's outback; follow by-roads faithfully,

Then you'll really know your Dorset.

Should you get lost – don't blame me!

(Editors note: Tollard Royal, on the border of Dorset, is actually in Wiltshire)

A Christmas Swan Song

Bernard Palmer remembers a festive prank

IN the years following the end of the Second World War, Christmas was something of a paradox. Air raids and fear were exchanged for relief and happiness but we still suffered deprivation as everything was rationed – including Bread which, even during the darkest days of the conflict, had never been controlled.

It was in this lean and hungry but carefree atmosphere that I, a 16 year-old apprentice boat builder with W & J Tod Ltd. at Ferrybridge, Weymouth, spent the lunch break on Christmas Eve with a group of other apprentices.

Swanning about and skylarking

In the course of our skylarking on the beach near the yard we discovered a dead swan. It was in mint condition so obviously had been dead for only a short time. As we examined it the germ of an idea formed in our evil young minds.

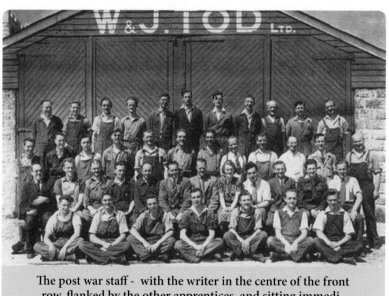

The post war staff - with the writer in the centre of the front row, flanked by the other apprentices, and sitting immediately before the Company owner, Mr. Norman Wright.

A Christmas Goose ! What a splendid caper !!

Amongst the staff in the yard was a middle-aged individual – I'll call him 'Fred' – who was a devoted supporter of Weymouth Football Club. He had been badgering us for weeks to buy tickets for the 'Terras' Grand Christmas Draw. Most of us bought one but on £1 per week apprentice's pay I certainly couldn't stretch to any more.

And so it was suggested that the newly found avian corpse was used as a fake prize in his draw

We quickly decapitated the bird and neatly covered the stump with a clean piece of hessian sacking and attached a brown paper label as above.

We arranged for the regular daily parcels delivery man to hand the now quite authentic looking bird to one of the Supervisors who, in all innocence, presented it to the 'Lucky Winner'.

Given the bird - to cook his goose

Fred was overwhelmed with delight and excitement, which our evil little group gleefully encouraged.

It was customary to close the yard a little early on Christmas Eve, and by that time we felt that perhaps we should come clean and let the poor man in on the prank. Just a small ruthless minority thought no harm would come by letting him 'cook his goose' but thoughts that he and his nice wife might succumb to a loathsome illness began to loom large.

Collectively we broke the news to him but he absolutely refused to believe us, claiming we were just trying to get the bird for ourselves.

At that point the hooter sounded and everyone clocked out with "Merry Christmas chaps" and hurried to catch their buses. Fred clambered aboard lugging the bird along and several of us got on, now desperate to remedy our mischief – but to no avail !

In the end two of us contacted a Supporter's Club Official and, confessing our misdeed, paid for him to go by taxi to Fred's home to confirm our story. I don't know what happened to the dead swan but Fred didn't speak to any of us lads for months. "What fools we young mortals were!"

A prize beyond price

Fred continued as a keen vendor of FC Draw tickets and, incredibly, a year or two later I won First Prize – a ticket to the FA Cup Final. One of the teams playing was Leeds United so my father, who was a Yorkshire man, was overjoyed when I presented the ticket to him. Leeds lost but Dad had an unforgettable day at Wembley.

A Day to Remember

A trip to the Festival of Britain by Peter Pitman

ON 30th May 1951 a group from Portland Secondary Modern School left Easton Railway at 7.15am bound for London and The Festival of Britain. We were sent off in great style and with a bang - fire crackers had been laid on the rails.

We picked up more trippers at Victoria Station, Underhill, and Weymouth, where extra carriages were attached, and Dorchester. Then on to London. We were each given a bottle of milk as we journeyed through the New Forest, some of us seeing the New Forest ponies and foals for the first time. Before arriving at Waterloo at 11.30am we had lunch - a meal of steak and kidney pie with potatoes and peas, followed by ice cream and wafer biscuits. What a treat!

We then made our way to the great event. First was the Lion & Unicorn Pavilion looking up at the Skylon, a huge, slender, cigar shaped tower anchored to the ground with steel cables. Then on to the Dome of Discovery where we saw many new inventions including a mock-up television studio with massive cameras and the set of 'What's my Line?' with the panel of Gilbert Harding, Lady Isobel Barnet and David Jacobs – models of course! Little did I think then that I would become an installer of televisions in the Portland and Weymouth areas when I grew up.

There were so many new and exciting things at the Festival to fire the imagination, including the first moving staircase, a visit to the Homes and Garden Pavilion where all sorts of modern furniture and household fittings were displayed, then stalls selling souvenirs and mementoes. I bought a lapel badge and a penknife which I still have. Would knives be for sale today, I wonder?

On the way out we passed the Guiness Clock which toured the country after the Festival and arrived in the Alexandra Gardens on Weymouth Seafront for us to go and have another look.

A very excited and exhausted party of school children made their way back to Waterloo Station and the return journey home, arriving at 9.15pm, after a fish and chip supper with ice cream and figs to follow. A wonderful day out, never to be repeated or forgotten.

The Skylon Tower

London and County Dinners

OF the Society of Dorset Men.   A short history by Hon. Sec. Hayne Russell

ALTHOUGH the first dinner, after the formation of The Society of Dorset Men in London, was held on 27th February 1905 at the Trocadero Restaurant in Piccadilly, there are known to have been at least two dinners previously organised for Dorset men living in London.

AT the Merchant Taylor's Hall on 8th December 1692 a number enjoyed what was called an "Annual Feast", suggesting that this might have been held previously for a number of years.

IN 1898 a dinner was held in the Whitehall Rooms with Lord Portman as Chairman, which was, in fact, the catalyst leading to the formation of the Society in 1904.

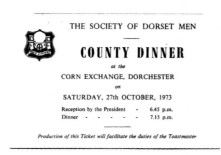

The inaugural dinner

In 1905 the company numbered 240, with Sir Frederick Treves in the Chair. As each member was introduced he shook hands.

The menu consisted of dishes reminiscent of Dorset, such as Portland mutton, a Dorset pudding, Dorset watercress and Blue Vinny cheese.

The order of proceedings for the evening set the pattern for all future dinners. These included the toasts "Dorset our County", "Dorset Men in London" and "Our Guests" with responses, a menu card which contained a number of dialect verses, the singing of

"In Praise of Dorset" and eminent guest speakers.

At this dinner a letter from Thomas Hardy, who was unable to attend, was read

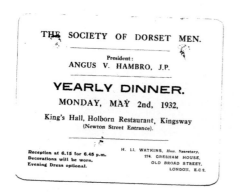

out and included the phrase "Who's afraid ?" – later to become the Society motto "Who's a'fear'd?" The speakers were Mr. Clavell Slater KC , Mr. Fossett Lock - The Mayor of Camberwell, and Sir Frederick Treves. There was entertainment involving dialect poetry and music.

A "men only" event

Undoubtedly the success of the first dinner established a tradition and the second dinner was held on 19th February 1906, again at the Trocadero Restaurant. The bill of-fare suggests that this was a feast of some proportion, consisting of a choice of two soups – clear pate d'Italie or thick St. Germain – a fish dish of boiled Ostend turbot, main course of boned sirloin of beef, a dessert of sweet Dorset pudding, followed by Pralinnee bombe and finally the Blue Vinny.

All the Dorset Mayors were invited and, although only four attended, this remained a tradition until the 1950s.

The third dinner saw a change of venue to the Holborn Restaurant and was held on Monday 6th May 1907 when 300 members attended. Comment was made in later reports on the physical task undertaken by Sir Frederick Treves to render a hearty handshake to everyone on arrival !

A presentation, of a silver tea and coffee service, was made to the Hon. Sec. William Watkins, who had been instrumental in the formation of the Society and in organising the dinners. A silver challenge cup was presented to Colonel Williams MP, to be competed for at the annual rifle meeting of the Dorset Volunteer Association. What happened to the cup remains a mystery.

Dinners then continued to be held annually at the Holborn Restaurant although the sixth dinner, due to be held on 9th May 1910, was postponed because of the death of King Edward VII and, because of the hot weather and probable lack of refrigeration, it was not possible to obtain any Dorset Blue Vinny.

By now the dinners followed a set pattern and, because of the number of speakers and the entertainment, they must have made for very long evenings.

A special distinction was given to the seventh dinner when, in response to the tribute of loyalty, a reply was received from the King. Given in Dorset dialect, as it always is, the tribute was sent by telegram prior to the proceedings and the reply received and read out later in the evening.

The tenth dinner on 4th May 1914 included an unusual entertainment in the form of a sword display performed by Lieutenant Wheeler of the Dorset Regiment.

Wartime and after

With the onset of the First World War the last dinner was held in 1915 and the Society reports stated "there were many who said it would be impossible to have a successful Dorset dinner in the middle of a war. Others declared the dinner was a necessity because at no other time had it been so imperative to keep the Dorsets together." Many who attended were in uniform and the speeches were full of calls for

patriotism and support for those members serving in the forces. It was reported that a "Comforts Fund" had been set up to send gifts to men in the trenches and to those who were prisoners of war in Germany. The Society had always maintained a close connection with the Dorset Regiment and the Commanding Officer of each battalion was an Honorary Member.

After the war the first dinner was known as "The Peace Dinner" and held at the Connaught Rooms on 5th May 1919. This was attended by several distinguished officers and amongst the speakers was Major General Sir Hugh Trenchard, later to be the first Air Chief Marshall of the fledgling Royal Air Force. Much praise was given to the exploits of the Dorset Regiment and the many members from "A'thirt the zeas" who had fought in the various campaigns of the war.

The London dinners continued as an annual feature in the Society calendar throughout the 1920s – held as near as possible to "Dorset Day", the first Monday in May. The Society flag always formed a backdrop with the County slogan "Vor Darzet dear the gie woone cheer" displayed above. The invitations, referred to as 'circulars' and sent to all members, were always in dialect and of some length.

Winston Churchill, one of the speakers at the 1925 dinner, having been detained in the House of Commons, arrived just as the Blue Vinny was being served.

Unfortunately there were vacant chairs at the 1926 dinner, specially organised to celebrate the Society's 21st year. The National Strike had prevented a number of members, especially from the County, from travelling. A special song was commissioned and sung at the event and for the first time the speeches were broadcast to the County by radio via Marconi's 2LO studio in The Strand.

Thomas Hardy never attended any of the dinners but did send his good wishes on a number of occasions in the early days.

One significant event of the 1930s was the vote taken at an extraordinary meeting of the Society on 28th April 1931 to simplify and shorten the title to The Society of Dorset Men. However the London dinners continued at the Holborn Restaurant. Reports are nonexistent for two years as no Dorset Year Books were published in 1933 and 1934.

Throughout the remaining 1930s the dinners featured the Band of the Dorset Regiment, playing from the gallery in the King's Hall.

The last dinner, prior to the commencement of WW2, was on 28th April 1939. The committee decided at the AGM in October that the blackout regulations made it impossible to continue.

In May 1946, there was a small gathering of members in the Connaught Rooms in Great Queen Street, merely to commemorate the dinner date. The first Society dinner after the war was held in the Connaught Rooms on 5th May 1947. The Lord Chief

Justice, Lord Goddard, was the main speaker and there was considerable consternation caused by a lack of Blue Vinny cheese because of rationing. It was back on the menu in 1949 when mention was made of organising functions "calculated to bring ladies into the picture". It was hoped that members would be supportive!

The 1950s

The new decade heralded another change of venue – this time to The Dorchester Hotel, Park Lane. In 1952 all the Members of Parliament for Dorset and seven of the eight county Mayors were present. In 1953 a Coronation Dinner was held and two of the speakers were from other County associations – the President of the Northumberland and Durham Society and the Chairman of the London Cornish Association.

The 50th anniversary of the founding of the Society was celebrated with a Golden Jubilee Dinner on 8th July 1954 and a special gold covered souvenir programme, including a history of the Society, was produced and signed by all those on "the top zettle" or top table. The President, Lord Llewellin, was unable to attend having been appointed Governor of the Federation of Northern Rhodesia, Southern Rhodesia and Nyasaland.

Another change of venue to St. Ermin's Hotel, Westminster was made in 1957 – also the year of a second yearly dinner; back in Dorset and at the Corn Exchange, Dorchester on 9th November.

Can ladies come too . . . ?

In the 1960s the London dinners continued to be held in May with the County dinner, now a permanent fixture, in November and moving to various venues around Dorset.

At the 1962 London dinner an extraordinary general meeting was announced to decide if Ladies should be admitted as members and invited to the London dinner. Both proposals failed but ladies were invited to the County dinner.

By 1970 numbers at the London dinner were down to around 60 – due, probably, to fewer members living in London and the growing popularity of the County dinner. Reports in the Dorset Year Book that had occupied six or more pages were reduced to two. Numbers of distinguished speakers were also reduced.

It was mainly through the enthusiasm and efforts of Hon. Sec. Gordon Hine and Toastmaster Roy Adam, placing their stamp on both events for a number of years, that the dinners again became well attended. Whilst the Dorset dialect had always been an important feature of the dinners, Roy Adam brought his own special brand of humour to the fore at these gatherings.

It's the Lord Mayor's show

The 1983 London Dinner took place in the magnificent surroundings of The Mansion House Egyptian Hall in the City, at the invitation of the Lord Mayor of London, Sir Anthony Jolliffe. Three hundred members, and ladies for the first time, sat down to a meal of traditional Dorset fare, many having travelled up from Dorset for the occasion. Time honoured traditions were followed and Sir Anthony, in proposing the "Dorset Our County" toast said "I am proud to be the 655th Lord Mayor of London and the first to greet The Society of Dorset Men to the Mansion House."

At the 1984 dinner, held at Simpson's in the Strand, Sir Anthony Jolliffe was congratulated on his elevation from Lord Mayor of London to President of The Society of Dorset Men.

Throughout the 1980s two annual Society dinners continued to be held. As numbers at the London event diminished the County function became more successful with eminent speakers again being a feature. In 1986 amongst those attending were Lt. Col. Gerard Boucher, aged 90 and celebrating 50 years as a member, and Capt. R W Annand VC. The Guest of Honour in 1988 was the High Commissioner for Australia, the Hon. Douglas McClelland.

Farewell London – attention Dorset

In 1991 only 41 members attended the London Dinner and despite the report "that it was gratifying to receive continued steady support" it was to be the last. After 86 years, excepting the war years, the London Dinners came to an end. Yet the success and popularity of the Dorset event, usually held in October each year, has grown consistently.

On Saturday 3rd July 2004, to celebrate the centenary of the Society, 300 members and guests sat down to a four-course lunch amid the magnificent surroundings of the HQ Officer's Mess of the Royal Signals at Blandford Camp, in place of the usual County Dinner. The toast to "Dorset Our County" was proposed by Vice-Admiral Sir Barry Wilson KCB who, in a splendid speech, took the gathering through a history of the Society with special emphasis on the military and its exploits in Dorset. The President, Sir Anthony Jolliffe, responded and said "There will always be a Society of Dorset Men as long as there is a Dorset."

For several years the County Dinner was held at The Crown Hotel in Blandford but the ever growing popularity of the event meant finding larger premises. After a trial period at Sherborne School the last three dinners have been held at The George Albert Hotel, just off the main A37 road between Dorchester and Yeovil, a popular venue that can seat 350.

We have been fortunate in recent years to welcome a number of well-known personalities as guest speakers, including Lord Chief Justice, Lord Philips – the Lord Bishop of London, Richard Chartres – Admiral Lord West of Spithead – Lord Guthrie of Cragiebank, former Chief of the Defence Staff - Col. John Blashford-Snell – and many others.

We should not forget our President, Lord Fellowes, who hosts the Dinners, welcomes the guests and whose presence is greatly valued.

STOP PRESS: *COUNTY DINNER 2014*

ON Saturday 25th October in the time honoured tradition, 189 members and their guests gathered at the George Albert Hotel, Warden Hill, Evershot for the annual dinner.

Despite the disappointing numbers attending, the dinner proved once again an undoubted success. The proceedings were presided over by our President Lord Julian Fellowes accompanied by his wife Lady Emma Fellowes and the guests were the Lord Lieutenant of Dorset Captain Angus Campbell, the High Sheriff Mrs Jane Stichbury CBE QPM DL, Lt General David Leakey CMG CBE and Dr Paul Atterbury Hon. DPhil BA(Hons).

The message of good wishes and loyal support from the Society which had, by tradition, been sent to H.M The Queen in Dorset dialect, was read out and the gracious letter of reply from the Queen read by the President. After the rendering of the dialect poem "Welcome to the Cheese" and to the strains of "To be Farmer's Boy" the Blue Vinny cheese was paraded for tasting by the President before serving.

The evening progressed with presentations by the President of the Hambro Golf Cup to Richard Harris and the Challis Cup for recruiting the most members to Trevor Vacher-Dean. It was announced that in future this cup would be accompanied by a small monetary award.

The toast to "Dorset our County" was proposed by Dr Paul Atterbury who is best known as one of the experts on the BBC Antiques Road Show. He described how he came to live in Dorset, how he loves its history, traditions and charm and that this is not appreciated. In particular, he mentioned Weymouth where he now resides and has no desire to live anywhere else. He believes Weymouth has much to offer and so much untapped potential with its harbourside, beach, Georgian seafront buildings and of course the Jurassic coast. He mentioned his involvement with the County Museum of which he said we should be very proud. He has recently been involved in the Sherborne Literary Festival and hopes to organise a similar event in Weymouth in 2015.

The next toast to "Our Guests" was proposed by Lt General David Leakey who is the Gentleman Usher of the Black Rod at the House of Lords. He gave an interesting description of the history of the office of Black Rod which was created in 1350 by Edward 1 and that it has a number of duties in addition to the best known role surrounding the opening of Parliament. These include dealing with disorder or disputes but rarely necessary, a security role which in the present climate has become very important and personal attendant to the Queen when she visits the House. In this respect he told an amusing story concerning being in the lift at the House with the Queen and the Duke of Edinburgh when it went up two floors instead of down much to his dismay. In this instant the Queen was possibly amused !

The evening was rounded off by the Chairman of the Society committee Stuart Adam who thanked the staff of the George Albert for the excellent service and meal. He then proposed the toast to the President who thanked everyone for supporting the event and said how much he had enjoyed another splendid occasion.

The M.C. was Mr Colin Fry who ably conducted the evenings proceedings.

The President welcomes his guests to the County Dinner (standing – left to right):
Guy Rich, John Stichbury, Captain Angus Campbell (HM Lord Lieutenant of Dorset),
Lord Fellowes of West Stafford DL (President of The Society of Dorset Men),
Lieutenant General David Leakey CMG CBE (Gentleman Usher of the Black Rod),
Sir Anthony Jolliffe GBE DSc DMus DL (Deputy President of The Society of Dorset Men),
Dr. Paul Atterbury Hon. DPhil BA(Hons), Stuart Adam (Chairman of The Society of Dorset Men),
(seated – left to right): Emma Jolliffe, Jane Stichbury CBE QPM DL (High Sheriff of Dorset),
Carola Campbell, Lady Emma Fellowes LVO, Shelagh Leakie,
Lady Georgina Jolliffe, Chrissie Atterbury.

DORSET – *the unforgettable*

by Kay Ennals MBE

In Dorset you'll find the unforgettable
seas that encompass soft, cool green vistas.

In Dorset you'll see indisputable
breathless scenery in such diversity.

In Dorset are villages so picturesque,
you will long to stay and wile the hours away.

In Dorset are records of histories,
of castles and dynasties, and ancient antiquities.

In Dorset you'll roam over meadows and hills
where rivers start springing and nature's full brimming.

In Dorset vitality fills fresh morning air.
A County so fair, there's none to compare!

Articles of interest, humorous or otherwise, prose or poetry, are solicited. All contributions must be voluntary and should be of a "Dorset" flavour. Contributions, with illustrations where possible, will be welcomed by post to the Hon. Editor, Trevor Vacher-Dean, at Rosslyn Cottage, 8 Love Lane, Weymouth – DT4 8JZ or by e-mail to vacherdean@yahoo.co.uk

Please ensure the correct postage is applied to all mail. Stamped addressed envelopes should be sent if mss or 'pictures' are to be returned. The Editor accepts no responsibility in case of loss and reserves the right to edit or condense contributions.

A Life in Art: Joseph Clark-Dorset Artist

By Eric Galvin, FRSA MA

ONE hundred and eighty years ago, Cerne Abbas was full of the news that Susan Clark had gone into labour. The household in Abbey Street was delighted when a boy was delivered safely on the 4th July 1834, but also fearful. Joseph was Susan's tenth child, but four older siblings died before he was born.

Joseph became a renowned oil painter who along with William Barnes and Thomas Hardy spearheaded Dorset's contribution to British culture just over a century ago. He specialised in pictures of everyday country life, many depicting children and some focussing on the special bond between the young and the elderly. The preponderance of indoor scenes makes it impossible to tell whether they report real incidents, people or homes in Cerne. His works have a strong narrative element with a positive take on daily life and offering hope to people in crisis. He exhibited 180 paintings at major exhibitions during his 60-year career including 107 at the Royal Academy. We know the titles of around 400 works and have images of about eighty.

He drew the inspiration for his work from his family life, education and strong Christian beliefs.

Watercolour of Cerne Abbas (1870) by Joseph Clark
Source Victoria and Albert Museum

Joseph's family

The Clarks were a large and well-known family. Joseph's grandfather came to Cerne eighty years earlier to repair the church clock and stayed to become one of the more prosperous tradesmen. He was a highly skilled long-case clock maker who in the 1790s opened a drapery business selling many goods including millinery and tailoring, and its own dowlas mill. This was a plain cloth used chiefly for aprons, pocketing, linings, overalls, shirts for workmen and heavy pillowcases. His daughters' marriages into well-to-do local families assured their future wellbeing.

William was a cultured man with strong social and business links in London. Several family members married in London, including Joseph's parents. The close bond with William Ellisdon's family deepened when Joseph's two brothers married Christiana Anne and Martha Ellisdon. Joseph knew London from an early age.

William Clark transferred his businesses to his sons in the 1820's and died in 1832. William Henry was clearly an enterprising man, making the best of every opportunity as Cerne's population grew and economy recovered from the slump after the Napoleonic wars. For example in 1837 he won the contract to supply clothing for 130 residents of the newly established Workhouse and others receiving 'outside relief'.

Joseph thrived and his earliest memories were of the town's two-day celebrations for Victoria's coronation in 1838. These included a thanksgiving service, a banquet in Abbey Street, open-air tea party and dancing. Joseph's favourite was the lighted candles placed in the window of every house as darkness fell.

Joseph's sister Charlotte Francis died in 1838 and further disaster struck in 1840 when his father died. His mother ran the business with her eldest son and the wider Clark family offered strong support. Following the marriage of Mary Susan, his older sister, and her departure for Christchurch, and the death of his remaining sister, Emma in 1852, there was little for his mother in Cerne apart from daily reminders of great sadness. She agreed that Joseph should go to London to train as an artist and accompanied him, living initially with the Ellisdon family. They stayed in London until the 1860s when Susan's declining health led to a move to Christchurch where she died in 1866.

After Joseph's marriage to Annie Jones from Winchester in 1868, they settled in Holloway in North London. In time, they had three children. In later life, he seemed to have been unsettled and they moved between the West Country and London. Although he never returned to live in Cerne, he visited relatives there for family holidays and play cricket. He retired to Ramsgate in 1917 and died there on his 92nd birthday.

Joseph's upbringing in Dorset contributed much to his practice as a professional artist as did his later family life in London's rapidly expanding middle class suburbs. He gained an intuitive feel for the plight of ordinary people facing great sorrows or living in poverty and responsiveness to demanding middle class clients. Family life and William Barnes' school turned him into a cultured man, vital for admission to the Royal Academy Schools(RAS).

Joseph's education and career choice

Joseph's elementary education was at William Bench's school in Duck Street. In 1845, Joseph became a boarder at William Barnes' school in South Street, Dorchester. The school's progressive curriculum and teaching methods turned boisterous boys into young gentlemen. He studied divinity, English, classics, geography, geology, and history; and took dancing lessons. As an adult, he read Shakespeare, Dickens and the Bible regularly.

After leaving Barnes' school, the question of Joseph's career arose. Though Barnes encouraged Joseph's interest in art, his family had doubts about the lifestyle and earning power of artists, informed by newspaper reports of the scandalous doings of the Pre-Raphaelite Brotherhood. Instead, Joseph went to St Neots to train as a retail pharmacist. He was home sick and unsuited to the trade. The family relented and he set off for London.

Joseph went first to Leigh's, one of the two main schools preparing aspiring artists for the entry examination for entry to RAS. Leigh's unconventional and progressive curriculum reflected the French atelier system.

In July 1854, Joseph became a probationer and in December he progressed to the Painting and Life Schools where he stayed for 2 years during which 13 leading artists known as 'visitors', supervised his progress. These included William Frith, Charles Leslie, Daniel Maclise and Richard Redgrave. He also attended lectures and sold small 'pot-boiler' paintings. During his time at the RAS, he gained valuable contacts with the leading lights in the 'genre boom' that swept British art in the 1850s. His formal art education nurtured his talents for accurate drawing and good narrative skills.

**Watercolour self-portrait from his student days
Source Victoria and Albert Museum**

Joseph's religious faith

Joseph's third source of inspiration came from his daily readings from Emanuel Swedenborg's spiritual writings. His parents belonged to the 'Swedenborgian' faith while continuing to worship at St Mary's in Abbey Street. When Joseph moved to London, he joined the New Church congregation in Argyll Street in St Pancras. In the late 1860s on returning to London, he became active in New Church life as a Sunday school teacher and governor of the Cromer Street day school.

He exhibited two biblical works but he generally demonstrated his beliefs in the responsibility of everyone to act kindly to those in need and the scope for finding comfort and hope in even the most distressing circumstances in genre scenes.

Joseph's artistic life and works

In 1857, Joseph received strong praise for his early works. The 'Dead Rabbit' shown at the British Institution was, unusually for a debut work, featured as a print in The Illustrated London News. This success continued when his 'The Sick Child' met made the tough standards set for the Royal Academy Summer Exhibition. Several national papers reviewed it favourably while the Sherborne Mercury said

> ' … we would draw attention to … "The Sick Child" of Mr Clarke … an exquisite family group, made of a loving tender father, pressing a sick child to his bosom… The homely grace of the mother … paternal anxiety … and other adjuncts of the picture are beautiful"

The paper made no mention of his Dorset roots and misspelt his name. 'The Sick Child' was the cornerstone of Joseph's reputation and appeared at international exhibitions in London International (1862), Philadelphia (1876), Glasgow (1901) and London's Franco-British Exhibition (1908). Other works went to the London (1862), Manchester Royal Jubilee Exhibition (1887), Melbourne (1892], Guildhall (1897), Earl's Court (1897) and Japan (1910).

Etching of 'The Sick Child' by
Joseph Clark (made 1858)
Source Victoria and Albert Museum

The first decade of Joseph's career was the most successful in terms of critical acclaim.

During the 1860s critical interest in genre declined, the emerging Aesthetic Movement attacked its basic approach and Joseph left London to accompany his ailing mother's move to Christchurch.

By the 1870s, the growing unpopularity of genre works in the artistic community had a direct impact on Joseph. In 1875, he became a member of the Society of British Artists but resigned two years later when James Whistler became its leading light. Later Joseph became associated in the public's mind with a long campaign about the way the Royal Academy's used the Chantrey Bequest originally intended to 'purchase works of fine art of the highest merit … executed within great Britain'. Sympathisers of the Aesthetic Movement argued that genre works were not of sufficient quality and the RA used the money to boost the income of Academicians and other favoured artists. They singled out Joseph Clark's 'Early promise'(1877) and 'Mother's Darling' (1885). The row ended in an inconclusive Parliamentary committee reporting in 1912.

'Mother's Darling' (1885)

In the 1880s, Joseph's confidence started to return and he became a member of the newly formed Society of Painters in Oil Colours where he exhibited 71 works until his retirement in 1916. He remained popular with the public and his works featured children's books, two Pear's Christmas annuals and advertisements for Bovril.

Whilst best known for genre works, Joseph also produced portraits, some of which he exhibited, and several documentary works towards the end of his career. In 1889 'Christmas Dole' portrayed the annual distribution of bread to poor parishioners at Hazelbury Plucknet, near Crewkerne, where Joseph was living at the time. The image on many Internet sites is really another work from 1902 by Joseph's acquaintance, James Clark. Other examples of documentary works include "War news at St Cross" (1899), 'Home from the War' (1902) and 'News from the Front' (1915). The First World War had a special meaning for Joseph as his son, Wilfrid served as a conscientious objector in the Royal Army Medical Corps in the Middle East.

Assessment of Joseph Clark's works

It is not easy to summarise Joseph's enormous output. Probably one of the best contemporary assessments came from John Heywood the Professor of Painting at the Royal Academy at the time of the Manchester Royal Jubilee Exhibition in 1887

'… There is only one specimen of Joseph Clark in the collection …It would have been interesting from an artistic point of view , and certainly conducive to our moral and spiritual welfare to have had a larger and more representative selection. … Joseph Clark is one of the most consummate artists living in all that appertains to the construction of a picture; he knows as well or better than any man living how to concentrate the interest his subject, and how to bring out its central point. There is no unnecessary detail, and yet nothing which helps the story is omitted. There is complete unity in his work; all the parts form a perfect whole. His pictures are full of concentrated thought and feeling - sweet, tender, and loving creations.

These characteristics appear in 'Family Worship (1911), a work typical of his output and used by Pear's Soap. It combines an indoor cottage scene, an amusing title, three generations, a clear narrative line and decorative detail.

'Family Worship' (1911)

For much of the twentieth century Joseph's works were, like other Victorian genre paintings, undervalued. There is a tale that when the teenage Andrew Lloyd-Webber approached his grandmother for a small loan to buy a Pre-Raphaelite painting she refused it saying that she would not have that trash in her house.

Seeing Joseph's works

Seven UK galleries have works by Joseph Clark but none is on display. The best way to see Joseph's works are as internet images though some of the images are poor and there are many misattributions. A good starting place is to search Google Images (or similar) for 'Joseph Clark British artist'.

Eric Galvin's book 'A life in Art –A popular Victorian artist and his world' will appear in 2016.   Contact him on eajgalvin@aol.com to make sure you hear of its publication. He also offers talks to local history, arts and other organisations about Joseph Clark and his paintings.   His grandfather was Joseph Clark's nephew.

A "Pearl of Wisdom" for a General Election Year

"ONE of the penalties for refusing to participate in politics is that you end up being governed by your inferiors." Plato circa 400 BC

The Dead House, Chiswell

A poem by Paul Snow

By the Cove House Inn at Portland is the old Dead House, although not called that now. It was a fisherman's shed for many years and then, after the Second World War, a boat store - but it had another use in earlier times.

"After storms and shipwrecks, bodies were dragged into the Dead House, and held there, to await their inquest and burial." – from The Book of Portland by Rodney Legg.

THE DEAD HOUSE

Behind the oak doors, torn and scarred by wind and years of driving rain,

a basket of mackerel, dead fish eyes staring in the half light.

Naked on planks,

half under rough sacking,

a dark curl of hair,

water and blood stuck to

white forehead,

a smooth arm blue green

and sea bruised

taking on the camouflage of fish.

Taken from the land and then taken by the water, returning to this –

half under rough sacking among baskets and pots, a tangled shroud of nets,

dead fish eyes staring in the half light.

An inspiring Aladdin's Cave or tarnished White Elephant?
This century Brewers Quay, the jewel in the crown of Weymouth's Hope Square, has certainly had its ups and downs, but Mike Ellery, the latest occupant, hopes that, despite continuing uncertainty, common sense will prevail. Giving the historic background to the site, he makes his case for Brewers Quay again becoming the major attraction for Weymouth, and Dorset, that it was not so very long ago.

BREWERS QUAY – THE PHOENIX ARISES (AGAIN!)

by Mike Ellery

"IT'S not like it used to be..." is the common cry of the current day visitor to Brewers Quay in Hope Square, Weymouth, the large red brick building that was once a brewery.

Formerly operated as a brewery by the Devenish dynasty, the way most casual visitors and indeed locals remember it is as a stunning, almost magical, indoor shopping centre, which finally closed in 2011. The Excise House public house with its indoor bowling alley has also been closed with the famous Timewalk, showing the history of Weymouth in various diorama forms-including the infamous recreated smell of the Black Death and the infamous talking cat!- and the Discovery, the hands-on fun area for children and adults alike. The many shops of diverse character included antiques, toy makers, delicatessen and ethnic wares from South America by Quipu.

Hailed as the Covent Garden of Dorset, the building is Grade II listed as from 1974. It was iconic and fantastic and put Weymouth on the tourist map but. . .

The History

Beer, it is claimed, has been brewed on or near the site since 1252, then in 1742 the brewery was built to take advantage of the nearby spring water from Chapelhay and the barley from nearby Radipole fields. Initially the brewery was owned by the Flew family but the Devenish family, brewers since 1642, purchased it in 1824 when three breweries occupied the premises. Davis Brewery closed in the 19th century, Groves continued until 1960 when incorporated into Devenish and beer was brewed there until 1985, when the site was purchased by Greenalls, another brewing dynasty. They had it for only three years before selling to brewing giants Scottish & Newcastle in 1998. Then in 2004 it was acquired by The Spirit Group, a breakaway group from Punch Taverns. By 2004 it had been offered for sale some fifteen times. Punch Taverns gave notice in 2007 for all shops and businesses to close down and leave. So the shops such as Arts Corner, Ship to Shore and Harbour Lights have all gone, allegedly to be replaced by an alternative wet weather attraction.

In 2010, under the ownership of a consortium of investors, known as Brewers Quay ILLP, based in Surrey, it was planned to transform the building into an 85 bedroom hotel, restaurant and luxury apartments. It was envisaged the Quay would become an upmarket development of housing and retail outlets. This was all to be ready for the 2012 Olympic Games. The closest this got was a few 'pop-up' shops which appeared for the Olympics but which closed soon afterwards.

It seemed that public opinion was much against the new plans because Brewers Quay was loved for what it was. Change is never welcomed is it? So it isn't "like it used to be..." and never will be again. Well it's not a brewery either is it?

In January 2011 planning permission was granted but so far little has happened. Plans have changed and the details are being rewritten and another planning application is being submitted. In March 2011 a huge number of the "one-off" exhibits - the essence of the uniqueness of Brewers Quay - were auctioned off in Dukes Salerooms in Dorchester and members of the public bought many other bits and pieces directly from the building. This signed the death knell of the way things were.

As it is today

In late 2012 a meeting was held with my associate Paul Cartlidge, Roger Doulton, a previous director, Alistair Ross of BQILLP and me in the offices at Brewers Quay. Paul and I put forward plans to rent large areas of the building in order to set up an antiques and collectables emporium. This opened on 28th March 2013. Later additions are a crafts area known as The Bazaar, the Art Asylum an exciting and very contemporary art gallery, a large furniture retail area,  containing antique and pine furniture by Martagon Antiques and painted furniture by Vintage Chic. The upstairs area also contains Stash Vinyl selling records and pop memorabilia, Floosie and Lush selling vintage clothes and offering upholstery restoration. We also have Peter Pope's vintage toy shop and Mike Bamber carving bone and stone. There are numerous smaller units including Wheely Welling vintage motoring items, Discobox selling DVDs, vinyl records and CDs; Forget-Me-Not selling vintage gardening items; Lou's Laundry offering vintage clothing and associated items; Dave Mauser and Trevor Pearson with stamps and postcards; Vintage Glitter and Shop 1.17 selling costume jewellery; Revived, Flutterbuys, Stash, Old Friends, Madelaine, Garamandas, Seaglass, Lin Manley-Hopkins, 1963, WAR, Glitz & Bitz For You and DH all selling general antiques, collectables and painted wooden items, Luke Woods offering bespoke photographs and Matty with Marvel Comic art . There is also a small cafe, Brewers Tea, on the premises offering a wide range of mouth watering food and drink. Artist and Photographic studios and a driftwood manufacturer have also been added along with a vintage bikers and antique shop known as Water Gypsies at the back.

The World War II D-Day museum at the Eastern end of the building and Il Porto Italian restaurant also opened and, along with the original workshops at the rear, the whole complex is going from strength to strength.

The building now houses the Weymouth Museum, which has been promised a space in any future development. The future is in the balance but we hope to be there for a few years yet.

A pipe-dream development?

In August last year BQILLP unveiled a new planning application to the public to include 3 bedroom houses, flats, and retail and restaurant outlets, plus plans to build

on the two car parks at the rear. A number of the great and good of Weymouth seem in favour of the new scheme but the public mood of "it's not like it used to be" seems to be the vogue and the prevailing feeling is that we cannot go through all this again with honest traders being thrown to the wall for the sake of a pipe dream development.

All this publicity of uncertainty has certainly not made it easier to attract business to the building but Paul and I will continue to do our best. We have been guaranteed occupation until at least September 2016 but are hoping for longer! This historic building needs common sense to prevail and hard working traders need to be left alone to ply their trade. Will this happen? Only time will tell.

To a farm labourer

A poem by Devina Symes

When I walked up the lane, he was always there,

looking over the gate, puffing on his pipe, deep in thought.

I would say "hello", and he would just nod.

Oft times he would come to the pub, sit quietly in the corner,

listening to the friendly banter of the locals, as he enjoyed his beer.

I never thought much about him, until I missed him at the gate,

his all consuming quietness, the worldliness in his eyes.

His eulogy revealed fortitude. A survivor of Flanders Fields,

returning to life on the land, content to be alive.

Your Genius Within

The latest motivational and inspirational book by Dorset author Barry Baines

EACH and every one of us has genius within - that is the assertion of local Solicitor Advocate and Master Practitioner with the Society of Neuro-Linguistic Programming, Barry Baines.

The answer to discovering your own strand of genius is to look inside yourself and work towards self-belief. Barry's book will guide you with anecdotes, assessments of personal values, learning strategies and exercises which really add a new dimension to perceived normality. Along with 34 hypothetical posthumous interviews with accepted geniuses, from many different fields and over millennia, this book aims to enable you to move forward with confidence, walk on the shoulders of giants and unleash your personal genius to burst forth upon the world. If this sounds a little 'over the top' - it isn't. Every page is worth reading.

This is a book for those who not only want to discover themselves but are prepared to work hard to find their genius within. "So long as you have breath in your body you have the opportunity to explore yourself in greater depth, and little by little the size of your genius will be uncovered."

This top self-help book, published by McLeod Moore, is available from Amazon as a paperback, to download as a PDF and on Kindle. ISBN 978-1-78407-153-0

RULES OF THE SOCIETY

(Incorporating the alterations passed at the Special General Meeting of the Society
held on 14ᵗʰ November, 2008)

NAME
1.   The name of the Society shall be "THE SOCIETY OF DORSET MEN."

OBJECTS
2.   The objects of the Society shall be:
       To make and to renew personal friendships and associations, to promote
       good fellowship among Dorset men wherever they may reside, to foster
       love of County and pride in its history and traditions, and to assist by every
       means in its power, natives of Dorset who may stand in need of the influence
       and help of the Society.

MEMBERSHIP
3.   The Society shall consist of a President, Deputy Presidents and Honorary
       Deputy Presidents if desired, Life Members, Vice Presidents and Ordinary
       Members.

QUALIFICATIONS
4.   Any person connected with the County of Dorset by birth, descent, marriage,
       property or past or present residence in the County, shall be eligible to be
       elected to membership.

MODE OF ELECTION AND TERMINATION OF MEMBERSHIP
5. (i)   The names of all candidates for election shall be submitted to the Committee,
         who shall have full power to deal with the same.

   (ii) The Committee shall have power to remove from the list of Members the
         name of any Member whose subscription is in arrear for 12 months.

   (iii) The Committee may also at any time in their discretion terminate the
         membership of any person without furnishing reasons for their action, in
         which event a pro rata proportion of the subscription will be returned.

SUBSCRIPTIONS
6.   The Subscriptions to the Society shall be:

   (a) Life Member - one payment £150.00
   (b) Vice-President - per annum (payable on the 1ˢᵗ October) £15.00

(c)   Ordinary Member- per annum (payable on the 1st October) . . .£10.00
These subscriptions will apply whether the member is residing in the UK or
overseas.

OFFICERS

7.   The Officers of the Society shall be:
Chairman, Deputy Chairman, Honorary Treasurer, Honorary Editor,
Honorary Secretary, Honorary Membership Secretary and Honorary
Newsletter Editor and they, together with the President and Deputy
Presidents, if desired, shall be elected at the Annual General Meeting each
year.
The Committee shall have the power to fill any vacancy arising during the
year.

COMMITTEE

8. (i)   The Society shall be governed by a Committee not exceeding twenty in
number, to be elected from the Members at the Annual General Meeting.
In addition, the Officers of the Society shall be ex-officio Members of the
Committee. Seven shall form a quorum.

(ii)   The Committee may delegate any of their powers to a Sub-Committee.

(iii) The Committee shall retire annually, but shall be eligible for re-election.

(iv)   Not less than twelve days before the Annual General Meeting the Honorary
Secretary shall send to every Member a notice of the Meeting. The Notice
shall also intimate to the Members that any two Members may nominate one
or more Members for election as Officers or to the Committee, and that such
nomination must be sent to the Honorary Secretary not less than four days
before the Meeting.

(v)   The Committee shall have power to fill any vacancy arising during the year.

MEETINGS

9. (i)   The Annual General Meeting will be held on a date to be decided by the
Committee.

(ii)   The Committee may at any time convene a Special General Meeting and they
shall do so within six weeks of the Honorary Secretary receiving a written
requisition signed by not less than twenty Members. Members requiring
such Meeting shall state in their requisition the subject or subjects to be
discussed, and the resolution or resolutions to be submitted thereat.
Notice of the date and place of all Special Meetings shall be sent by the
Honorary Secretary to each Member twelve clear days prior to the date fixed
for the holding of a Meeting, and such notice shall state the object or purpose
for which such Meeting is convened.

BOOKS AND RECORDS TO BE KEPT

10.   Proper Books of Account, showing all receipts and expenditure, shall be kept

by the Honorary Treasurer, and the Honorary Secretary shall record and keep Minutes of all Meetings of the Committee. The Membership Secretary shall record and maintain a list of members.

EXAMINATION OF ACCOUNTS

11.   At each Annual General Meeting two Examiners shall be elected to examine the Accounts of the Society for presentation to the members at the next Annual General Meeting.

ALTERATION OF RULES

12.   These Rules may be amended, altered, or varied by a majority of two-thirds of the Members voting at a Special General Meeting.

COMMITTEE CHAIRMAN: STUART ADAM

Court Barton, West Bagber, Taunton, TA4 3EQ. Tel: (01823) 432076
Email: stu.adam@outlook.com

Members of Committee:
P. ASHDOWN, G. KING, S. CREGAN, A. HUTCHINGS,
A. PROWSE, J. ROUSELL, P. SNOW, S. WOODCOCK

OFFICERS:

Hon. Secretary: H. C. RUSSELL,
34 Brunel Drive, Preston, Weymouth, DT3 6NX. Tel: (01305) 833700
E-mail: hrussell@gotadsl.co.uk

Hon. Assistant and Membership Secretary: P. LUSH
25 Maumbury Square, Dorchester, DT1 1TY. Tel: (01305) 260039
E-mail: peterlush3@hotmail.com

Hon. Treasurer: I. MORTON
1 Wainwright Close, Preston, Weymouth, DT3 6NS. Tel: 01305 832722
E-mail: ianvalmorton@fsmail.net

Hon. Editor "The Dorset Year Book": T. VACHER-DEAN
Rosslyn Cottage, 8 Love Lane, Weymouth, DT4 8JZ. Tel 01305 781261
E-mail: vacherdean@yahoo.co.uk

Hon. Newsletter Editor: M. L. HOOPER-IMMINS,
2 Waverley Court, Radipole, Weymouth, DT3 5EE. Tel: (01305) 779705
Email: hooperimmins@btopenworld.com

Society Archivist and Historian: REV DR J. TRAVELL
44 Cornwall Road, Dorchester, DT1 1RY. Tel: 01305 264681
E-mail: johntravell@outlook.com

IN MEMORIAM

The President and Members mourn the loss of the following worthy
fellow Dorsets and tender their sincere sympathy to their relatives.

W T G PERROTT (Bridport) MIWO	Hon Life Member	10/10/13
(Past Hon. Sec. of Society)		
G V GOULDING (Poole)	Ordinary Member	2012
GORDON FOOT (Langton Matravers)	Ordinary Member	12/1/11
CLIVE POULTER (Wareham)	Ordinary Member	14/1/14
TERENCE LOVE (Wareham)	Ordinary Member	1/11/13
SIR STEPHEN HAMMICK (Wraxall) OBE DL	Ordinary Member	15/2/13
SQ LDR P CHERRY (Childe Okeford) ACIB	Vice President	28/12/13
DEREK CLARKE (Milborne St Andrew)	Vice President	July 2013
PETER MARKS (Ferndown)	Ordinary Member	May 2013
CAPT DENZIL PERRY (Childe Okeford)	Ordinary Member	Dec 2013
ALAN JOHN COLLINS (Swanage)	Ordinary Member	13/4/13
DON E COX (Weymouth)	Ordinary Member	March 2014
MAJOR MICHAEL ALLARD (Bryanston)	Vice President	19/5/14
JOHN LEACH (Weymouth)	Ordinary Member	13/5/14
ARTHUR J MONK (Weymouth)	Vice President	29/6/14
ROYSTON J TEE (Dorchester)	Vice President	15/7/14
SIR JOHN COLFOX (Bridport)	Ordinary Member	July 2014
ROBERT D J OLIVER (Swanage)	Ordinary Member	14/6/14
DAVID J TRICKEY (Dorchester)	Ordinary Member	15/8/14
(Ex Chief Supt, Dorset Police)		
DAVID JOHN FOX (Christchurch) OBE DL	Vice President	6/5/14
(Ex Mayor Christchurch & Co. Councillor)		
WILLIAM OSMOND (West Stafford)	Ordinary Member	21/8/14
ROBERT HURST (Swanage)	Ordinary Member	9/9/14